RETURN TICKET

The crew of the Messie Bessie
Standing, from left: 2nd Lt. David Shoss, navigator; 2nd Lt. Carl L. Svendsen, bombardier; 2nd Lt. Warren LeBaron, co-pilot; 2nd Lt. George L. Roth, pilot.
Front row: S/Sgt. Harry E. Rulong, tail gunner; S/Sgt. Burl L. Reynolds, top turret gunner (engineer); Sgt. Glen J. Allen, left waist gunner; S/Sgt. Carl R. Carlson, right waist gunner (back-up engineer); S/Sgt. Paul E. Hunter, ball turret gunner; S/Sgt. Willie B. Yates, radio operator.

Return Ticket

My Diary as a POW Airman in WWII

Carl R. Carlson

2001

Copyright © 2001 by Carl R. Carlson
All Rights Reserved

First Edition
Second Printing

A Geron & Associates book from
The Watercress Press, San Antonio, Texas

Graphic Design by Lenella Meister

For additional copies:
Carl R. Carlson
6 Clermont Ct.
San Antonio, TX 78218
(210) 822-3558
caruranch@earthlink.net

Library of Congress Control Number: 2001097749
ISBN # 0-934955-45-X

For my grandchildren,
Elizabeth, Aeyrie, Andrew, Kaylie,
that they may learn what happened then
and for my crew mates and fellow prisoners,
who know

ACKNOWLEDGEMENTS

It was at the urging of my family—particularly my daughter and son—that I have unearthed the diary I kept as a Prisoner of War in Germany during World War II and put it in book form. From my capture on June 24, 1944, to liberation almost a year later, it was only my faith in God and thoughts of my family in Texas that kept me alive and sane, despite the miserable conditions of imprisonment.

The lessons I learned from this experience make me especially appreciative of the love and devotion of my family of today. My thanks go particularly to my wife, Ruth, who has performed the tedious preparation of the manuscript from my diary, as well as the gathering and sorting of photographs and documents.

For my daughter, Patricia, and son, Stan, and their own children, I am eternally grateful for their love and consideration, and my fervent prayer is that they never know the horrors of war in any form. May they always honor their country as I do, and pass on to succeeding generations a firm understanding of what freedom means.

Carl R. Carlson
9 September 2001
San Antonio, Texas

CONTENTS

Prologue xv

PART ONE—The Capture 1
   June 24, 1944
Early Morning Interrogation and Another Truck Ride . . . 11
   June 25, 1944
   June 26, 1944
   June 27, 1944
In Paris 13
   June 28, 1944
Leaving Paris by Rail for ? 14
   June 29, 1944
   June 30, 1944
   July 3, 1944
Transient Camp 17
   July 4, 1944
On the Move Again 19
   July 5, 1944
Deeper into Germany 21
   July 6, 1944
The Sirens Start Screaming 25
   July 7, 1944
Goodbye Berlin 27
   July 8, 1944

PART TWO—Stalag Luft IV 35
Camp Life Begins 35
   July 9, 1944
   July 19, 1944
   July 21, 1944
Time Goes By 38
   August 7, 1944
   August 15, 1944
A Loaf of Bread 40
   August 30, 1944
   September 7, 1944

Fighting for Bread 42
The Red Cross Comes Through 44
   September 14, 1944
   September 28, 1944
Midnight Shakedown 47
   October 6, 1944
   October 16, 1944
   October 24, 1944
   October 26, 1944
A Surprise 51
   October 31, 1944
The Dogfight 52
   November 1, 1944
   November 3, 1944
   November 4, 1944
What About Mail ? 54
   November 6, 1944
Athletic Equipment 57
   November 10, 1944
   November 12, 1944
A Sunday Sermon 59
   November 14, 1944
   November 18, 1944
   November 19, 1944
Christmas in Captivity 60
   December 5, 1944
   December 6, 1944
   December 17, 1944
   December 24, 1944
   December 25, 1944
1944 – Is It a Year to Remember or to Forget? 67
   December 31, 1944

PART THREE—The New Year 69
January 1, 1945
January 11, 1945
Good-bye Stalag Luft IV 70
January 15, 1945
January 22, 1945
January 23, 1945
The Russians Are Coming and We Are Going 73
January 30, 1945
The Test of Tolerance 75
January 31, 1945
February 3, 1945
February 4, 1945
February 5, 1945
Arriving at Stalag Luft I 78
February 7, 1945
Our New Home – Stalag Luft I 80
First Mail at Stalag Luft I 89
March 4, 1945
March 9, 1945
Good News 96
March 12, 1945
Crop Planting Time in Texas 98
A Shot and a Parcel 99
March 16, 1945
March 21, 1945
March 23, 1945
March 27, 1945
Easter Sunday in a POW Camp 100
April 1, 1945
April 24, 1945
Camp History 103
Good News Keeps Coming 105
April 30, 1945

PART FOUR—Liberation 108
The Goons Are Gone 108
    May 1, 1945
Day Two of Liberation 111
Day Three of Liberation 115
Day Four of Liberation 116
    May 4, 1945
Day Five of Liberation 118
Day Six of Liberation 118
Day Seven of Liberation 119
Day Eight of Liberation and Still Waiting 121
Days Nine, Ten, and Eleven of Liberation 123
    May 13, 1945
The Planes Are Coming 125
On Our Way 126
    May 14, 1945
Camp Lucky Strike 127
The Waiting Game Goes On and On 128
Departure Day 129
    June 11, 1945
My Trip Home 130
    June 12, 1945
    June 20, 1945
    June 21, 1945
Epilogue 135
Targets Bombed 137

ILLUSTRATIONS

frontispiece The crew of the Messie Bessie
Author Carl R. Carlson xiv
Membership in the Caterpillar Club was earned the hard way . . .3
My prison dog tag 37
Cigarettes from the Red Cross gave me writing paper 46
The wonderful first letter from home 56-57
My parents on the farm 58
The "cigarette diaries" I kept hidden in my mattress 94-95
Cover and page from my prison diary 110-11
My POW record from Frankfurt which I found near Barth . . .113
The telegram telling my parents I had been liberated 129
Carl Carlson and David Shoss, San Antonio, 1987 136
Carl Carlson and Glen Allen, San Antonio, 1987 136
The Luckye Bastardes Club recognized my survival of the
    POW experience 138
Chaplain's Letter 139

RETURN TICKET

Author Carl R. Carlson

Prologue

This is late spring in the year 1944. I am in England at our B-17 bomber base located at Thorpe Abbotts. We are situated approximately 90 miles north of London and I am remembering some of the events that have happened to our B-17 crew.

On June 6 the ground invasion of Germany took place, and World War II is in full bloom. It looks like the war with Germany has now turned to favor our side.

Our crew has been flying bombing missions for several weeks at a steady pace and it almost seems like routine, but it is still scary. We know there is a real danger of being hit by flak or enemy fighters. We have witnessed this on every mission. I believe we will be the lucky ones to make it through the war without being shot down. Our entire crew believes it won't happen to us, and that gives us courage.

As a crew, we know that we are helping to win this ugly war. I find courage and faith are needed more than anything else. This makes going on with my duties as an airman much easier. Just knowing there is a God and He is watching over us gives us comfort.

At this time our crew of the 100th Bomb Group in the 418th Squadron has flown twenty-four bombing missions in our assigned B-17 plane named "Messie Bessie", Tail Number 42-30152-D.

Planes are lost every day and some crews are shot down on their first mission, so you can see why our crew feels that we are lucky. We have been hit by flak and enemy fighters several times but we have not been severely damaged.

There was one serious injury on our second mission. The bombardier, Svendsen, was hit in the jugular vein by flak and almost lost his life. The navigator, Shoss, kept his hand over the wound, slowing the bleeding, and this action saved Svendsen's life.

We are scheduled for six more missions and that will be the end of our tour. The thirty-mission requirement was raised from twenty-five only a few weeks ago. Six missions more don't sound too bad and we feel we will surely make it without any problems.

There are at least two reasons for the increase in the number of missions. One is we are losing many planes and replacements cannot come in fast enough to relieve us. The second reason is that the average mission has been shorter since D-Day.

Many more targets are now in France and Belgium at this time, but we are still making runs in Germany and they are the most dangerous. Germany is where most of our planes have been shot down.

A "milk run" is what we call an easy mission with little or no opposition. We have had several targets in this category and it is always good news when we are told we are going on a milk run. It is not guaranteed to be easy, because many crews have been shot down on a so-called milk run, but your odds are much better.

We know we must be prepared for anything at all times, on short or long missions. Most of the missions are scheduled early in the day and that means we must rise very early, usually from two to three hours before take-off time. We have to dress properly, eat breakfast, go to the mission briefing, and then we have a few minutes with the chaplain for a short prayer before taking off. All of this takes time, so it's not like jumping out of bed and into your car and off you go to work. Careful planning is done to prepare for each mission.

Part One
The Capture

June 24, 1944

This is Saturday morning, June 24, 1944, and it appears we will not be flying today as we were told yesterday that the 418th would be on standby. That means we cannot leave the base this weekend because there will be no passes, but more than likely we will not be flying a mission today. This is a good morning for some of the men to sleep in.

Most of the crew is caught in bed when we get the word to prepare for a mission. We can hardly believe what we are hearing because it is past the time that we normally have to be ready for take off. We are told we have two hours to be at the plane. This will be enough time, but we have to move on quickly for a late breakfast.

When we get to the briefing room and look at the map, we see this is a milk run, so maybe our Saturday midday run will not be very long or difficult. We have been told we will have no problems with fighters or flak if we stay on course. Our target will be a V-1 rocket airfield near Rouen, France.

Within 30 minutes after briefing, we take off, not in a B-17, but in a truck. We have been told our regular plane,

"Messie Bessie", is still in repair because of the numerous hits we received June 18 on our 23rd mission. We had a close call at the target near Brunsbuttelkoog, Germany. The plane we used yesterday is on a mission with another crew. We journey a short distance by truck to the 390th Bomb Group to borrow, if you will, another plane.

As we approach the plane it looks almost new and the name is "Return Ticket", Tail Number 42-97065. The name looks good to all of us, because we want to return to this base in "Return Ticket." After warm-up we take off and join our 418th squadron. We arrive at the French coast and everything is going well. In the distance we notice an undercast of clouds that is not supposed to be there. The weather report we received at the briefing said no clouds. Because of the cloud cover the target cannot be found. We are flying at about 22,000 feet and the pilot has just said over the intercom that we are looking for another target because the clouds are covering the area we are supposed to bomb. The clouds are broken here and there.

The search for a new target has been going on for quite a while and all of a sudden flak is spotted up ahead. We start throwing out chaff. Chaff is strips of aluminum foil that scrambles the radar on the flak guns so they will not fire accurately. This has happened to us many times before, but it is not supposed to happen on a milk run. The flak is getting closer and it is more accurate as all of our planes have exhausted their supply of chaff.

The Germans can, and probably will, start tracking us with ease. The flak guns are quite accurate tracking with their radar. Puffs seem to be getting too close for comfort. Then someone from the front reports flak at 12 o'clock level. I am getting quite concerned, but this has occurred before and we were not hit. Surely this time it will be no different. Our bomb run has not even begun and the flak is so close.

Now we are preparing for the bomb run, so I suppose a target has been found for us to bomb. This is, and has always been, the most dangerous part of any mission. We are like sitting ducks.

Finally bombs away and just at that moment we are hit directly on the number three engine. The engine is gone and we are on fire. The flames are going back as far as the tail of the plane on the right side. Outside of my window, in the waist-gunner area of the plane, I can see flames.

My first thought is to grab my chute and snap it on as we all know this is a severe hit and things look extremely bad. Everything is happening so fast. I don't believe we can make it back to our base even if the plane doesn't explode. Now the fire has almost gone out, except for the area around the lost engine. The plane is very hard to control and the pilots know we are in deep trouble so orders are given to bail out. It is like we are all on a roller coaster as everything is whirling around fast. Time is an important factor in saving lives, so I yank the safety pull from the waist door and it flies off like it is supposed to do. Without any hesitation I jump out head first. I hope not to hit the tail section of the plane. Without stopping to think I grab for the chute pull cord almost as soon as I

Membership in the Caterpillar Club was earned the hard way

clear the plane. I want to know very quickly if the chute will save my life. It does open, but not without a very, very severe jerk, and it feels like my back is breaking. I thank God that the chute did open and I really didn't mind that fast stop.

My thoughts reflect on a pledge I made to myself that I would never bail out of a plane—I would take my chances on the plane making it to a safe landing. That quick choice I had to make was quite easy considering the condition of our plane. I have seen many planes go straight down after being hit and the crew had no chance to bail out. This could have happened to us. When orders were given by the pilot to bail out, out I went on the double.

So here I am on this Saturday afternoon hanging in midair and there is dead silence. This is an unbelievable change from all of the noise a few moments ago. Things have changed from chaos and confusion to absolute silence. It is so quiet that I don't even want to say a word to see if I can hear my own voice.

It seems like there will be plenty of time for thinking. I really can't tell if the chute is dropping or going back up. My concern now is for the other crew members as the plane is nowhere in sight. It just vanished and I don't see any other chutes.

Now I have spotted three chutes in the distance. Objects are quick to disappear—all of a sudden the other chutes have disappeared. At least I know that four out of ten bailed out safely.

I can see the waist door sailing downward and it is far below me. It is tumbling over and over and I can see a flash when the sun hits the side of the door. At times I can see the ground through broken clouds and smoke from what appears to be the target we bombed. Hopefully our target was hit so this will not all be in vain.

I never thought it would be so difficult to gather thoughts. There are just too many things going through my mind. There seems to be plenty of time for thoughts and prayer. I pray that God is with me and that He will see me through this ordeal. It is encouraging to have faith and to know that prayers are answered. I do believe God will take care of me at this time.

The waist door keeps flashing in the sun as it is dropping much faster than this chute. Sometimes it seems the chute is going back up as the wind currents change. Now the door has disappeared and I assume it is on the ground. This will be a souvenir for someone.

It doesn't seem like I am going down very fast because everything below looks so small. The wind currents must be playing games up here. Am I really going down or just hanging up here? I keep thinking it is taking too long to get down. This could be good and it could be bad. It is probably bad as this gives the Germans more time to watch and figure out where my landing will take place.

We were flying at 22,000 feet and it does take a while to descend. These are very anxious moments, to say the least. This is one time it is impossible to know what is going to happen when this all ends on the ground. It is very difficult to be positive and to think that something good is going to happen; in fact, I am certain it will be the opposite.

My mind has shifted from what has happened to what is going to happen. This is really the unknown. We have been told that if we are captured to reveal only our name, rank, and serial number. That is all that I can remember right now. After all, this was not going to happen to our crew.

I do believe the ground is getting closer and I am getting very tired of hanging up here. I am not comfortable and this ride has to end sooner or later. I must face what is to come when I hit the ground. Hopefully the ground is what I will land on, and not in a tree or in electrical wires. There are many trees and the ground does not appear to be very level. I can see a river in the distance and I could land in the water and that might not be too bad. At least I wouldn't break any bones.

As the ground gets closer, the many trees are evident and there are some houses and barns in the distance. Now I can hear small-arms fire in the distance and this is the first sound I have heard since bailing out of the plane. It appears they may be shooting at one of the other crew members. I now see the three chutes I saw earlier. They are not shooting at me and I am thankful for that bit of good news.

Now the ground is coming toward me very fast, and it seems like it is coming to me instead of me going to the ground. They say you can pick your landing spot, but this parachute is not a sporting model and it looks like it will pick its own spot to land. This will be a potluck landing. It is evident I will not land in the river I saw earlier. The ground is close and I will also miss the trees. I don't want to get hung up in a large tree.

My landing spot is on a hillside and it is a rather steep slope. As I land I know right away I have a problem because my left foot caught most of the weight on the hillside. My ankle is hurt very badly and I believe it is sprained or fractured. This is unfortunate because I thought it might be possible to hide or escape from the Germans. These thoughts end now as I cannot put any weight on the foot.

It appears the French people have been watching the chute come down because many have gathered around me. They all seem to want to help, but they also seem to be very afraid. Two French ladies do speak English and they are concerned about my situation. They tell me they want to help, but cannot because they are afraid of being caught by the Germans. All of the faces seem to be sympathetic. They are apologizing for not being able to do something for me. We have a few minutes to converse before the Germans come. They ask me my name and where I am from in America. I tell them I am Carl Carlson from Texas.

My capture must be close at hand as the French people seem to be backing away as if afraid. A short distance away I see a German vehicle that looks like some kind of an open jeep, and it is coming very fast with the dust flying. Thinking fast, I give my assigned pistol to the French girls because there will be no chance for me to use it and it could cause a problem when I am searched. I am sure the German soldiers are thinking, "We can't let this one get away." Unfortunately there is not much danger of that happening because this foot problem takes care of trying to escape. I am a sitting duck for them.

They pull up in their vehicle and quickly jump out. The two young soldiers, probably 18 or 19 years of age, point their rifles with fixed bayonets at me. I hope they know they are not supposed to hurt a captured American soldier. Let's also hope they know about the Geneva Convention and how to treat prisoners of war.

I try my best to tell them that my foot has been injured as they are making motions for me to get up fast with my hands in the air. They seem very cautious and demanding. One wrong move and I will not get out of this situation alive. They have finally figured out that I have a foot problem. They motion for me to get into their vehicle, but I can't move without help. Now they are searching me thoroughly. They take my wallet (it contained no money), watch, Air Force sun glasses, and all of my personal items, but of course they do not find a pistol. After the search, they help me get into the vehicle.

I really do regret leaving the friendly French people who are just standing there staring. These two German soldiers are very cocky and seem elated that they have captured an American airman. I am sure this will be a star in their German crowns. Some of the French people are slowly waving as we leave. Those long faces I will never forget. The French people have their hands tied as one wrong move on their part and they will not be around very long. They are completely controlled by the Germans.

We start moving and travel a short distance, probably two or three miles, and arrive at a small German Army headquarters. Here I am told to get out of the vehicle. Some German officers arrive and this is rather frightening as it is unpredictable just what they will do. They do speak English and surprisingly they are acting a little friendly. I am searched very well again, but everything that I had was taken away from me by the first search. The only thing I have left is my clothing and flight boots.

As this is taking place I see four of our crew members, Allen, Schultz, Hunter, and Rulong, coming in, and am I glad to see them . . . but sad to see them in the same situation.

This seems to make each of us feel better to know that at least five of us survived by bailing out of the plane. I hope we will soon find out about the rest of our crew.

All five of us were picked up in the same manner and we do not have much to smile about at this time, but we are grateful to be alive. We are all searched again by different officers. It seems that they want to make sure they have done a good job of searching. Now comes the interrogating and they are actually telling me what bomber squadron I am in and they want me to verify this information. I only tell them my name, rank, and serial number. I will not answer any questions or verify any statement made by them.

My foot is hurting and it feels like a balloon in my flight boot. It is getting very tight in the boot and is quite painful. They have ignored my foot completely. I cannot put weight on the foot and it will be difficult to walk without crutches. Schultz also has a slight foot injury caused by the parachute landing, but he can hobble and put some weight on his foot. Schultz has only flown a few missions with us as he is a relief person. He, along with several others, has been taking the place of our crew member Svendsen, who was severely injured by flak, as I mentioned.

I am sure we will not see the other crew members here and we will not know their fate for a long time. This is agonizing for me because I want to know about the entire crew.

We are a close-knit group, flying together for a long time. We flew training missions together before we made the twenty-five bombing missions. The pilot, Roth, and co-pilot, LeBaron, are the best to be had. They are very careful, level-headed, and they are liked by our entire crew. I do not know of a disagreement or problem among our crew. This was not always true with other crews. Some had personnel changes many times and therefore they did not get to know each other very well. Training together and flying missions together can make a big difference. That is the case with our Roth and LeBaron crew. We know we can rely on each other no matter what problem or emergency situation occurs. This is a good feeling. As time went by we became like a family and this is why we are very concerned about the other half of our crew members.

The day does not seem to be over as far as traveling is concerned. We are being loaded into a large canvas-covered truck with the rear end open and wooden benches around the sides of the truck. We are joined by several other American soldiers who have also been captured. We cannot communicate because we are being watched by six guards. There is a guard for each two prisoners. We have to be very quiet under these circumstances.

Most of the orders are given in German and they expect us to know what they are saying and to follow their orders. Where are they taking us this late in the day? How long will we be in the back of this uncomfortable truck? Evidently they are taking us to a place of safekeeping for the night.

We are stopping at a German Army camp and it looks like they just want to show us off to the soldiers at the camp. We must be some kind of a valuable catch or maybe they have not seen American soldiers before. This is really building their ego to see us captured. I am sure that is the whole idea. At this point I feel very, very small and defeated and my foot is hurting so badly I feel ill. The German soldiers believe they are winning the war. They are very cocky as they come by to take a look at their "prize catch."

The news has spread because many Germans are now coming by for a close look at us. The German soldiers here look mean. We are now beginning to move on and I am glad to be leaving this place.

We have been traveling for what seems like a couple of hours and it is beginning to get dark here in France. I think the clock would show that it is quite late in the day. We seem to be arriving in a large city. Maybe this will be our stop for the night. I have just found out that this is Evreux and we are being taken to a regular jail for safekeeping tonight.

We are given individual cells for the night and finally offered a small bite to eat. I am not even hungry, and it has been a long time since breakfast. I will eat a little because I have to keep going. This ends the first day as a German Prisoner of War. It will be difficult to sleep tonight. I have never slept behind bars before. The pain in my foot and ankle is severe. My boot is still on and I probably would not be able to remove it even if I tried.

Early Morning Interrogation And Another Truck Ride

June 25, 1944

Yesterday was a very long day and it was like a bad dream, but that has to be put aside for a while. What is important now is what is going to happen today because this is a very uncertain situation. It was hard to sleep in this place last night. I am in jail guarded by Germans and they are the enemy. These things they call beds are not comfortable, but I suppose they were not built for comfort like ours back at the base. These beds are for criminals and that is what we are in the eyes of the Germans.

This is not an ordinary morning as it seems breakfast is not first on their schedule. I am very nervous and concerned. Interrogation comes first this morning.

No consideration is given to my foot and it is a real problem. With assistance I am taken into an open area, like a courtyard surrounded by prison walls, to be interrogated. Their questions are very familiar, and some are not questions but statements that they want me to verify. I am again shocked to hear some of these statements. They tell me my squadron, group, and my base in England. I will not even so much as nod my head.

Have you, as a child, ever been questioned by your parents and you made up your mind that you were just going to sit there as if you heard nothing? That is what I am doing at this time.

The interrogator gets irritated and upset because he is not

getting the answers he expects. He is not exactly losing his cool, but he is quite irritated. He acts as though he might be reprimanded by his superiors if he does not get me to talk. He tries a bit rougher approach—a pistol is placed on the small table between us. It seems I have become very stubborn, but this new approach doesn't bother me too much. I trust he surely is not going to use the gun. (The gun was not touched.) I should mention that the interrogators are very fluent in the English language and they seem to be well-trained and intelligent officers.

I am now back in the cell and have received what they call breakfast. This is one time in my life I wish I could understand German. It is difficult to follow orders you do not understand, especially when you are expected to follow their commands immediately.

It has been several hours and I realize we are not going to stay here any longer. It is time to "Rouse!" and that means to move on. I am beginning to understand some German. We are not far from the American lines and I feel sure they want to get us as far from our lines as possible.

We are being loaded into the German trucks and this time there are several trucks as the number of prisoners has increased. We are well guarded and we don't try to converse with each other. Our group consists of both American and British prisoners.

It is now late afternoon; it was around noon when we left Evreux. I am sure we are going away from our American lines here in France.

After riding in the truck all afternoon, we arrive in Chartres. Here we are in another prison that is not much different from the last jail.

June 26, 1944

We are still in Chartres and it appears this is a holding place until further plans are made. We are just waiting to see what happens next.

June 27, 1944

It is now late in the day on our fourth day of capture and we are being assembled and prepared to move on to our next destination. I see fellow crew members at a distance and this is very uplifting. We are not always in the same truck because there are several vehicles carrying prisoners.

I feel sure we will all end up together at the same camp, even though we are not being transported together. I need help boarding because I still can't walk on my left foot. Hanging on the shoulders of buddies is the only way I can navigate.

The guards here are not as impatient as the others have been. I am thinking some of the German soldiers may have a little compassion, but the guns with bayonets are always at their sides.

In Paris

June 28, 1944

Early this morning, we arrive in the city of Paris. We can only see out of the back of the truck as the rest is covered with canvas. It appears we are going straight through the center of the city.

Finally, after anxious moments, we come to the railroad yards and we are again placed in a nearby jail.

I suppose we will be here until we are put on a train to who knows where. I realize these are the railroad yards that we have bombed. It is one of the regular targets for our Air Force.

Paris is a hub for transporting German military supplies to the front lines and that is why it is considered a major military target.

This is the first time I feel we might be subject to yet another danger. I hope Paris is not a target for tonight. Our fighter planes regularly strafe the supply trains arriving and leaving Paris.

As the day goes on we hear air raid sirens often. This is very scary, but we are lucky today because no strafing or bombing has occurred at this location.

The time has come for us to take a train ride. We are given time for a comfort stop before loading. This is a rest room like none of us has ever seen. There is a large open room with no toilet seats or urinals. It only has hand rails and a hole in the floor. You have to squat down and then use the hand rail for assistance to get up. Have you ever tried to squat down on one foot and go to the bathroom? The hand rails makes this operation possible . . . but barely. What an experience this has been today.

Leaving Paris by Rail for ?

We are leaving Paris at night—I assume to avoid the American fighter planes. A moving train seen by our fighters is a sure target for strafing or bombing. This is a passenger train, or a least the part we are in is for passengers. The seats are made of wood and it is not comfortable, but who said we are to be comfortable? We are at least sitting down.

It looks like most of the guards on the train are German officers along with a few enlisted men. The majority of the enlisted men are probably on the front lines. I have heard some of the officers speak English and I am sure this is a requirement for their position.

Once in a while we can say a few words to the person next to us when the officers are not looking. We are not supposed to converse with each other, but it is nice to talk now and then when we have the opportunity.

We have been moving all night. This seems to be the plan—to move at night and avoid any day movement that would attract the British and American fighter planes. Our fighter planes are always on the lookout for moving trains.

It is difficult to sleep because the seats are very uncomfortable, it is hard to sleep in a sitting position, and my foot is giving me a lot of pain.

June 29, 1944

This is a new day, and I assume we are still in France, somewhere between Paris and the German border. It looks like the rule of traveling at night has been changed because we are still moving and it is daylight.

Now the train has stopped and I wonder why. The German guards are practically screaming at us and at each other as if they don't know how to handle a situation. We realize there are fighter planes above and it appears they have spotted us. The guards are afraid to leave the trains without the POWs, and they are somewhat confused.

Now the officers have finally decided they are too afraid to stay on the train to face the possibility of being strafed by our fighters. We are commanded to leave the train at once. It is everyone for himself. It is not easy for me to move fast by myself, but this has to be done and to each his own. I finally end up crawling into the woods because it is impossible to jump on one foot wearing heavy flight boots. The pain in my foot also makes me feel weak.

The guards have stationed themselves behind trees in a semicircle to keep us from escaping into the forest. The trees also give protection in the event of strafing. As there are a lot of trees I have found one to hide behind, and I hope I am on the back side in case of strafing. No one knows from what direction the fighters will come, but at least the tree gives some protection.

This episode is soon over and we are not strafed. Orders are now given to get back on the train and some of my buddies are helping me. I was hoping the train's engine would be hit to make it immovable, but this was not to be our luck today.

If this ordeal had not been so serious it would have been funny. Seeing the enemy act as human beings was amusing. Up to this point we had our doubts about them. They were really in fear of their lives. They have the same fear about being killed in this war as we have. It seems this was a totally new experience and it nearly threw them.

The fighter pilots must have been looking for a more vital target today and we are thankful it was not this train. Now we know why it is not wise for the Germans to move supplies during daylight.

Because of the near strafing the officers have decided to stay where we are for a while. Some trains are passing on their way to Paris while we are on a side track. They are taking a chance of being strafed. As I have said before, trains standing still are not a great target; the moving trains should be a hot target for our fighter planes.

We started moving again late today and we are meeting many troop and supply trains that appear to be headed for the front lines. They all seem to be in a hurry. I know for sure we are heading for Germany as we see many trains coming from that direction.

June 30, 1944

I was figuring Germany must not be far away, for this is our third day on the train, and now we find out we are in Germany and have been here for a day or two. It is hard to know exactly where we are located because we are still not moving during the day—just traveling at night.

July 3, 1944

After five hard days of traveling on this train we have stopped in a German town and we are ordered to get off. It looks like our numbers have increased so we must have picked up more POWs along the way. I wonder what is going to happen to us now?

Transient Camp

This stop here in Germany seems to be different from the others. Many thoughts go through my mind quickly as to what is in store for us. Is this the end of the line? Will we stay here for the duration? There are no military trucks here so that means no transportation to our next destination. At least there is no worry about luggage or anything to carry. This is what you call traveling very light. We have only the clothes we are wearing and nothing in our pockets.

Since there are no trucks, we start walking. The train is now leaving us behind. Again I must ask for assistance from my friends to keep up with the group. I do not see anyone else who is in need of help. So by putting my arms on the shoulders of two buddies, I hobble on the good foot and try to keep up with the formation.

Surely this cannot be a very long walk, but it is beginning to seem endless. I know that my helpers must be getting tired. Now others are offering to take turns helping me hobble. I am grateful for these kind buddies.

It appears we are approaching some kind of a prison camp. Again there are no trucks. They must need them for moving troops and equipment to the front lines. Word is getting around that this is a transient camp and we will just be here temporarily.

There is no welcome mat out for us, and the first order of business is another shakedown. This must be at least the fourth time. They seem to be concerned about objects hidden in our clothing. The search is very thorough. As far as I can tell there is no chance we could have anything hidden on our bodies.

The next item on the agenda is another interrogation. This game is going exactly like the first time I was interrogated. The officer speaks very good English so you cannot say you do not understand what he is asking. He uses extreme pressure and he gets upset and angry when you refuse to answer his questions. I again give only my name, rank, and serial number. He attempts to frighten me by shouting in an extremely loud voice and displaying a pistol within his reach (but not within my reach).

Many questions are asked that I could not answer even if I wanted to or if my life depended on it. The officer gets tired of hearing my name, rank, and serial number. This seems to really irritate him as it means he has failed to get the desired information.

Now the interrogation is over for this time.

This camp is not a jail and it appears to have been built to hold temporary prisoners. I have found out that we are close to Frankfurt, so we are in the heart of Germany. Unlike the jails in France where we had individual cells, here I share the room with several other prisoners.

July 4, 1944

Today is July 4th and what a place for Americans to spend such an important day. There seems to be an unusual amount of commotion this morning. We have been ordered to get in line for something, but we don't know what is going on. Surely it is not another interrogation, because we usually don't line up for interrogation. Something else must be happening.

Now that some of our buddies from the front of the line are coming back we learn they are taking our prisoner-of-war pictures and getting our fingerprints. They are also completing some sort of a personnel file on each one of us. This will be a picture that I won't care to see. My appearance has probably changed, and not for the better. Who cares what this picture will look like as I will probably never see it anyway.

My army serial number is printed on a cardboard and put across my chest as they take the picture. Now I suppose I am properly labeled.

On the Move Again

July 5, 1944

We have been here two days and we are now preparing to leave the camp on foot. The same routine for helping me walk is needed and my good buddies are here again to give me assistance.

We have probably walked about two to three miles, but it seems much farther under these walking conditions. Now we are back at the same location where we got off the train two days ago.

On the train we go again. My foot still bothers me and I have had no medical attention. The flight boot has not been removed and my foot is very uncomfortable.

This is getting to be a tiring trip. It seems it will never end. How long will it be? This just can't go on forever as it has been ten days since we left Evreux. Germany can't be that big unless we are going in circles.

As we travel deeper into Germany we are not only traveling at night but also during the day. The chances of being strafed by fighter planes has decreased because we are far away from England. The Germans evidently feel safe deep in their homeland. What they really must fear now is heavy bombing in the larger towns and vital military targets such as factories, airfields, and oil storage depots.

Traveling on the train, out in the country, it is hard to believe there is a war going on. As I sit here in the uncomfortable rail car I find I have some thinking and meditating time. I am concerned about my family and wonder if I am listed as missing in action or if my family has been told I am a POW. I am concerned about the rest of our crew members and how the war is progressing.

The train does not go very far without stopping, so evidently there is other business going on besides handling the American and British POWs. We are allowed to keep the shades up so we can see the countryside as we travel. This is not the case at night when the shades have to be closed and we are blacked out. This, of course, is to prevent detection by aircraft flying missions. Most of the night flights are done by the British Air Force. Maybe the ride will be only one day as it seems we are causing the enemy much trouble.

I guess they have plans worked out for us because now we are ordered to get off the train. This time there are trucks waiting to take us to our next destination. The truck ride is short because we are already approaching another prison camp. Could this be where we will stay for the duration? We can't ask questions so we will just have to wait and see what happens.

Turns out this camp is not much different from the place we just left except the guards aren't bothering us here. It always makes you nervous when they call on you to come with them because you are wondering what they are going to do to you this time. Word has gotten around (and I have no idea how word gets around here) that this is just another transient camp. It is possible some of our POWs are of German descent and they understand what the guards are saying. That may be why we get information by the grapevine. I don't know if the rumor is good news or bad news. If we move it will mean getting on a train again and that doesn't sound good to us because we are very tired of trains.

It seems we are getting ready to do something different as I see trucks lining up for us to be loaded to go somewhere. We have stayed here two days and two nights, and I have learned it is called "Wetzler Transient Camp."

Deeper into Germany

July 6, 1944

Another train ride and the cars are equally uncomfortable.

This is a passenger car, or it is supposed to be a passenger car but there are no cushions — they are hard wooden seats. It is good to have a rather thick and heavy flight suit to give a little help on the hard seat. I wonder how long this flight suit will have to last and how long the boots will stay together. The Germans are not concerned about giving us clean clothes, or having us remove the dirty flight suits. It has been thirteen days and we have not had a shower or a bath during the entire time.

We are rolling along now, but as usual we make frequent stops. Each time, I wonder if this will be our stop to get off of the train. Even though we are deep into Germany, the rule is to roll down the curtains early in the evening. It is bad when we can't see out of the window when we are moving and stopping.

Today we are ordered to keep the curtains down most of the day and that means the lights are on inside. The lights have to be on so the guards can watch our every move. One guard is stationed at the front and another at the back of the car. They are always standing so they can observe what is going on at all times. We have been ordered not to talk to each other.

We have arrived at what appears to be a large city. As the shades are partially open we can see this is a huge railroad yard. It seems much larger than the yards in Paris. Could this be Berlin?

I just found out that it is Berlin. This is a target we have bombed and I have seen several of our bombers shot down here, with the fate of the crews unknown. There was so much antiaircraft flak when approaching the Berlin target we thought it would be impossible to get through without getting hit. Most of our planes did make it, but there were always unlucky ones shot down. We were fortunate when "Messie Bessie" bombed Berlin because we didn't receive major damage.

I will never forget the time I saw two planes go down. One got hit and made a nose dive, out of control. There was no chance of anyone bailing out. The other plane exploded when it was hit. No one could have survived or even bailed out as chutes are not worn while flying. We have to grab and snap on our chutes when we are ordered to bail out.

The train has stopped in the middle of the railroad yards and I hope not for long as this is a very hot target for American and British bombers. It looks like we will be staying here for a while because the engine has gone.

I believe the number of prisoners in this car is about fifty or sixty. We are very anxious because the shades have been ordered pulled down. There are no German guards inside the car and it looks like we are stranded here for the night. All of the lights are out and it is very dark. We are extremely crowded and everyone is quiet. It is scary, to say the least, sitting in the middle of a large railroad yard locked in a lonely car in a prime military target.

It is time to pray and I hope my prayers will be answered, "Dear God don't let the Berlin railroad yards be the target for tonight because we are sitting ducks." This is where my mind starts spinning. I am thinking about what has happened in the past days and what will happen in the future.

There has been a change in our position. We are now sandwiched in between box cars and this is good as it will give us some protection in case of bombing.

It is getting too dark now to see anything out of the cracks in the shades. I can hear train engines switching and moving constantly. We are in the middle of a very active marshaling yard.

The guards are bringing us a little something to eat now — a slice of dark German bread. Now the guards have left, but you can be sure they are watching us from the outside. There is no need to even think about escaping unless you want to get shot. Sleeping tonight will not be easy.

We are all hoping our stay here will be very short, but it looks like we will be here tonight. Who knows if it might be for longer. We are in a very dangerous position. Since the guards are outside the train, at least we can talk without being watched.

My crew buddies, Allen, Rulong, and Hunter, are close by and it makes me feel better to talk to them. We talk about our concern for the rest of our crew members. We do not have the answer as to what happened to them and we may not have an answer for some time. As I have said before, we feel almost like family members. We trained, made twenty-five bombing missions together, and now we are prisoners of the Germans. Our group is close knit and we have concern for each other. We talk about how thankful we are to be alive, but we know there is still danger in this terrible situation. We feel that God will watch over us during this ordeal.

The guards are now back inside the car and I think it must be around midnight. The lights are very dim and there is just enough light for the guards to watch all of us. The shades are closed and this will be a blackout night. We are hoping that the blackout works so our planes will not bomb us tonight. We have to be quiet, so it is time to see if I can sleep in a sitting position. I hope no bombing is scheduled for tonight.

The Sirens Start Screaming

Suddenly the most unbearable sound I have ever heard blasts our ears. It is the air raid sirens. I am guessing that it is about 4 A.M. and the first thing that I notice is that the guards are leaving. Now they are locking the doors and they seem scared and we are scared too. What a terrible sound. It makes you want to dig a hole and crawl in where it would be safe.

Several minutes have gone by and there is no sound of planes and no bombs exploding. It could be the alert is given far in advance or maybe we can't hear the planes because of the sirens.

Now all of a sudden the rail car begins to shake and I hear the sound of bombs exploding, but it is in the distance. I thank God that this is not the target for tonight. The target is probably a factory or an airfield near Berlin. We are all relieved at this moment because this rail yard has been spared and the lives of American and British POWs have been saved. It is a good feeling to know the British Air Force was so close and doing their job to help end this war.

There must be an all-clear because the guards are back on duty. They are very quiet and so are we. I have a feeling that after the air raid, the guards are really angry with us because they know most of us have been on bombing missions over Germany.

July 7, 1944

As daylight appears, through the sides of the shades I can see the railroad yard is back to its usual amount of activity. Train engines are still roaring close by and there are a lot of trains switching. I am wondering when I will feel that bump that tells the hitch on our car has been connected and we start rolling.

I have realized that this is an important day in my life. It is my 22nd birthday. What a way to spend a birthday! I haven't mentioned this to anyone. I had hoped we would have finished this trip by today, but it appears this wish will not be granted.

The Germans seem to be in no hurry for us to move from this place. Possibly this is a collection point for more accumulated POWs and they want to make this a worthwhile trip with a full load.

It is about noon and the bump we have been waiting to hear has just occurred, so hopefully this means we will be on the move. We don't want to be here another night to find out if Berlin is scheduled for another air raid. We hope to get out of here quickly. Even the guards seem excited about leaving. I suppose they also had a frightening night.

More cars are being added so I feel sure a freight or passenger train is being made up for us to begin our trip. As we start to move we keep wondering where we are going. Will this trip end soon?

I am getting very tired, as you can imagine. It has been fourteen days since our capture and we are getting smelly and not too easy to get along with, but we have to try to be patient. We are beginning to look like bums instead of members of the U. S. Air Force. My foot is some better although the boot has not been removed and I still cannot walk without help. All of this seems to be of no concern to the Germans. Their job is to hold on to their catch and keep us from escaping. We are still well guarded and we know the consequences if we try to escape.

Goodbye Berlin

As we leave the Berlin area it is almost a happy occasion because it is less dangerous away from the large cities. That is not to say the train could not be strafed or bombed, but the chances are less likely this deep in Germany. As far as I can tell there are no war supplies being transported in this area.

We have been given permission by the guards to raise the curtains and it is good to see the outside once again. The country is beautiful. We are in the forest area of Germany and it is unique. We are making many stops, but most of them have been short. The train goes fast at times, and then it will slow down. We have no information about where we are going, but we do have a new set of guards and a new officer in charge. They came aboard in Berlin. The officer speaks broken English and he understands every word of our English.

The new officer has said nothing about talking, but we feel it is best to keep our conversations quiet and low-keyed. This place has many ears as the guards are always alert and listening for information of importance.

Another day seems to be coming to an end and this is our fourteenth day, and I call it a miserable trip. It seems another night has to be spent in this rail car. At least tonight we should not be in danger of an air raid and bombs. It is getting dark and precautions are still being taken to be sure all curtains are down and the lights are dim.

We are moving and I hope we keep going. The countryside seems to be blacked out from what I can tell from the sides of the curtains.

We have to remember we are in between the east and west fighting fronts. We are wondering, since we are going east, just how far we are from the eastern border and the Russians.

I have been reflecting on one year ago and remembering that our crew had not even been formed a year ago. I had not completed gunnery school, and had not attended flight training. I guess things have been moving fast this past year. Here I am in this unbelievable situation. It goes to show you life is very uncertain. We don't know from one day to the next what will happen, but we have to strive to overcome the problems we face each day. It is not easy to make the adjustment to the situation we are in at this time.

July 8, 1944

This is the fifteenth day of captivity. We are moving at a slow pace now, surely this has to be the last day of the train ride. Germany can't be that large, but we probably have not covered many miles each day.

I am irritated, miserable, and tired of the whole ordeal. Being raised in a home where my Swedish mother scrubbed the floor and everything else each day, this filthy situation is hard to take. Again I have to tell myself to be calm as that is the best way to stay out of trouble. Prayer helps me more than anyone will ever know. No matter what happens to me I will always be able to pray. Prayer and thoughts of my loving family are what keep my hopes up at this time.

It will be a relief to reach the POW camp. I hope we will be left alone and not harassed by the guards when we get to the camp.

It looks like we have arrived somewhere at last and would you believe, we are given the choice of walking or riding. Now I see only the injured are permitted to ride. I am riding and it seems that we have traveled about one or two miles.

Now we are being unloaded from the trucks, and it appears we will wait for the walkers to arrive before we are permitted to enter the camp. It shouldn't be long, but there is no need to hurry and I hope we have arrived at our final destination.

One thing that makes the ordeal hard to accept is not knowing how long we will be in the POW camp. How long will it be before we can win this war? The Germans feel they surely will win and they act like they have no doubt about it.

We are not talking much to each other at this time because there is just too much going on, and my mind is in a whirl.

We are still waiting for the walkers. I can see the gates, barbwire fences, and barracks up ahead where we will soon be going. We are obviously not the first POWs to arrive at this camp. There appear to be many others who have had the misfortune of being captured. Now we realize where many of our other crew members have gone after being shot down. It is good to know that many of our men did make it to this place and did not lose their lives.

At last the walkers are arriving. They are not walking like soldiers but just dragging along. After the long train ride they do not have any extra energy. I hope we are through riding trains. This experience is something I do not care to repeat.

There is no cause to be energetic. We are waiting for the

gate to open. Our group of POWs is large—I estimate it to be around two hundred soldiers. This tells me that many of the stops we made along the way were to pick up additional POWs.

The gate is open and we are being herded like cattle into the camp. Friendly greetings are being received from POWs already confined in the compound. Many quick questions are asked by our new friends even before we are given instructions as to what to do next. Our friends are asking, "What is your group, squadron, where were you shot down, and how is the war going?" Questions and more questions are asked until we are ordered to move on down the line. The Germans are not through getting the necessary information from the new arrivals.

It looks like we are going to have a briefing, but not an "I am glad you are here" speech. I think we are getting a "German sermon" from a short, redheaded hot-tempered Gestapo officer. He isn't talking—he is screaming his message to us. I don't know what he is trying to tell us. I would just as soon not know as it seems to be a lashing of some kind. One thing for sure, I can tell he is angry at the world and especially unhappy to see us arrive. I feel sure he would have preferred us shot on sight rather than taken as POWs. I hope we will not have to see this camp commander or listen to what he is trying to tell us any more after today.

There is concern as to what the conditions are going to be like in camp with this officer in charge. It is even difficult to think of him as a member of the human race. I hope his subordinates are more compassionate, or we may be in deep trouble.

We are being searched thoroughly and again we are being

interrogated. There are no new questions for them to ask.

This is the place we get rid of the filthy flight suits. The new clothes we are given are from the Red Cross. Even though my flight suit is soiled, I almost hate to part with it. There are no new shoes, but in my case I can't get a regular shoe on or my flight boot off. My foot still hurts and the flight boot is very tight on the left foot.

I believe they have started the room assignments. I am sure this will take a long time because they are also completing room records.

I want to tell you about the camp. The enclosure is called a compound and it looks like there will be more compounds, as I see construction going on in the distance. There are ten barracks plus a couple of extra buildings. One building looks like an assembly hall and there is a large outside toilet. The toilet has a roof but is open at both ends. It contains about forty seats and a long trough that extends from one end of the building to the other. The building is twenty-five to thirty feet long. After I have had the need of its use, I will tell you more about the great open-air toilet.

The conditions here seem to be extremely crowded and they say more POWs are coming in daily. It will not be long before it is filled to its capacity.

Each barracks has ten rooms and each room has twelve bunk beds located around the walls. There is one window in the barracks with outside shutters. One stove is near the middle of the room, and there is no furniture except for the bunk beds. We have no easy chairs, but then this is not supposed to be like home. At least it will be much better than the railroad car. I can stretch out on the so-called bed at night. You can't really call these things beds, but I haven't figured out another name for them. The mattress is a straw sack. It is burlap, partially filled with straw, and that is not so bad. The bad part is that the straw sack is placed on five wooden slats. I can feel all five slats when I lie down. Oh well, just one more adjustment that has to be made. I was hoping at least one of my crew members would be assigned to this room, but no luck. There is no such thing as trading places with someone in another barracks. I will have the opportunity to get to know all twenty-three roommates very well.

My left foot is slowly getting better and the swelling is going down. I can now apply some pressure on the foot, so hopefully I will be walking on it soon.

We have had no food today and the hunger pains are getting rather severe. It is a little hard to be yourself when you are hungry and there is no food in sight.

It is afternoon on the first day here so we don't know what is on the menu for dinner. The news isn't very good as our new buddies say, "You won't get much to eat."

Now we find out they are correct. Each room is given a two-gallon bucket. At this point I didn't know why we were given a bucket but we soon find out that one person from each room is to take the bucket to the building I called the assembly building, where each bucket is filled with boiled potatoes. This is to be our first meal at Stalag Luft IV. One bucket of boiled potatoes divided between twenty-four hungry men! How do you divide one bucket of potatoes between twenty-four hungry men?

This is our first major roommate conflict. We finally get the potatoes divided, but I can see a problem developing if this is going to be the way we are fed. The potatoes are no doubt the best potatoes I have ever eaten and everyone here agrees. They have no salt or butter, just plain boiled potatoes. One bucket of potatoes is not enough for twenty-four hungry men, but this was all we had for our first and only meal today.

We all agree that whatever we get to eat must be divided equally among all of us and we must figure out how to do this so it is fair to all; otherwise, we will surely have problems. Tempers are much more likely to flair when you are hungry. I have said before, you are not yourself when hunger pains are present.

In our barracks we have five rooms on each side, divided by a hall that goes to the outside doors. There is a small emergency washroom at the end of the building, containing a couple of urinals and two seats. This is for night use only as the doors to this facility are locked during the day when we are outside in the compound.

The main doors to our barracks are locked from the outside very early in the evening. We are locked in for the night. The shutters on the outside of the windows are also closed. According to what the others who have been here for a while say, we are locked up every evening at about 6 P.M. and doors are not opened until around 8 A.M. the next morning. This makes a long, long night in a stuffy room.

I understand the compound is filling very fast and it is sad to know the Germans continue to shoot down many of our planes. That is bad news for me and all of the others here in camp. Stalag Luft IV is for non-commissioned Air Force officers only. We have both British and American airmen here. God only knows where our commissioned officers are being held.

I drew top bunk, which is all right with me except it is rather close to the ceiling so I have to watch my head. I have found that if I shift some of the straw in the mattress towards the shoulders it helps because the legs can do on less padding.

One thing we must all do is adjust to the situation we are in under these conditions. I have made it this far and will make it through this ordeal no matter what happens. Life is too valuable to let it slip away here. I have faith this will be over some day so we can all return home to our families and country.

Part Two
Stalag Luft IV

Camp Life Begins

My room number is Two and I am in Barracks Eight which is located close to the outside latrine I mentioned earlier. We have been told again that the inside toilets are to be used only at night. The number of men in each barracks is 240, so you can see how inadequate two commodes are for our needs. The water supply is also limited, so the toilets are to be used only in an emergency. There are a couple of shower heads in the emergency room, but the water is usually off and there is no soap. Maybe this tells us something. No salt for the potatoes and no soap for the shower.

We are learning fast about the conditions here. The lights go off early in the evening. They lock the doors and then about two hours later the lights are turned off. The shutters are closed at the time the doors are locked.

July 9, 1944

It is now Day Two and we have already guessed there will be no breakfast. I was hoping we would get lunch but "no lunch" was the word. It is evening and we get our bucket of potatoes. There is a lot of grumbling about this very sparse amount of food; maybe it will get better.

This morning the door was unlocked around 8 A.M. and the first thing on the agenda was to fall out by barracks and line up in formation. We didn't know what this was all about as several officers were involved in this operation and they were speaking German so those of us who do not understand German didn't know what they were saying. Now we know that they are counting us. They are very careful as they call each one of us by name. They want to make sure that no one has escaped. This took at least one hour and we had to stand still and be quiet until they were satisfied no one was missing. We were dismissed after a short lecture in English.

It was good to be outside in the fresh air, to see clouds and the sun. These things I used to take for granted. When everything is going well it is easy to forget how important the small things in life can be. What used to be small things look like big things now.

As we were excused from the formation we were at least free to stroll within the compound. We spent a lot of time talking to fellow POWs.

We are surrounded by high barbwire fences and I can see the guard towers and machine guns. There is a warning wire about twelve feet inside the high wires and I see security dogs outside. I believe they have us very well secured. There is no chance of escaping from here as I observe at this point. We were told as we entered the camp about how grave the consequences are if anyone tries to escape. You will be shot on sight if any attempt is made and I believe they mean what they say.

We are called "Kriegies" by the guards and our camp is approximately two and one half miles south of Kiefheide which is located in the Northern Pomerania sector of Germany. Stalag Luft IV was activated in April of this year and it has not been completed.

We have been issued a "Kriegie" dog tag to be worn at all

times. My number is 2809. Our American dog tags were not taken away from us, so we are wearing two dog tags.

The medical infirmary has two doctors and it is located in a small part of a barracks. It contains a few beds for emergency cases. With many soldiers coming to camp, some have serious injuries that need medical attention. There are also many other ills, so the two doctors are kept very busy.

My prison dog tag

July 19, 1944

The doctor has looked at my foot, as all of the injured were ordered to report to the infirmary, and now they have me confined. I am not sure where the two doctors are from, but they are not Germans. They are probably British. I have been told I need to start walking on my foot and they will assist me in the beginning. I have put on a regular shoe that has been given to me by the Red Cross. They do not have x-ray equipment here, so they cannot determine exactly what damage has been done to the foot. The skin on that leg is a very dark purple, but there are no visible signs of broken bones. I have been assured it will heal and should not cause too much of a problem in the future. This has been a two-day stay and I am glad to find out that the foot will continue to improve.

July 21, 1944

As I have stated before, this is a new camp as it was opened in April of this year. Most of the area is still under construction, so it seems they plan on bringing many more POWs here.

A Swiss delegate from the Red Cross has been here inspecting the facilities and I understand one of the major complaints —second to the shortage of food—is the ventilation at night in our rooms. Everything is closed tight and it does get stuffy. We have been told the Germans have promised to improve this situation in the near future.

According to the Geneva Convention agreement, delegates are to be permitted to inspect the conditions of all POWcamps. They in turn tell the German officers in charge of their findings. The food situation was brought to their attention and it seems they promised things would improve. The Germans, knowing the delegate won't be back for some time, are promising improvement as an easy out. Maybe the Germans could care less about all of the prisoners, but I really hope this is not the case.

We are pleased that someone from the outside is allowed to come in and observe the conditions here in camp and make recommendations. We will see what the results from the visit will be and we hope it will be good.

There are several German soldiers in the compound we call "goons." They appear to be ignorant because they slowly walk around the compound with their hands clasped behind their back. They are not armed and we suspect their mission is to listen for information. The word is out for us to keep our conversations low key when they are near by. We have also noticed all of the goons are short in stature.

Time Goes By

August 7, 1944

Several weeks have passed and I realize how slow the time is going by and what a boring place this has become. It is August and I have been here a month so I have learned what to expect. This compound seems to be full.

When we are locked up at night, we occasionally detect unusual noises coming from under our floor. Others have noticed the same thing. The barracks are about three feet off the ground and there are large doors outside for entry under the building. We suspect the goons are under the floor listening to our conversations. It seems they are still trying to pick up information that could be useful to them in this war. So again the word has gone out for us not to talk about our organization or any military information during the evening while locked in our rooms. We can talk when we are outside during the day. The goons have been known to come into the rooms during the night and pull a POW out for interrogation because of conversations heard in the room during the evening hours.

The outside toilet, or latrine, is not built for comfort or privacy. It is open on both ends and the seats are about 40 holes cut in wooden boards. The wooden holes sit back to back. There is no sewage system, but there is a rectangular concrete holding tank. About once a week the goons pump out the sewage. They add water to the mess, attach a large flexible hose, and start pumping. What sounds like a large one-cylinder engine is used to suck the sewage into a portable tank. They haul the portable tank away to who knows where and we have a clean toilet for a little while. The sewage removable operation is very interesting to watch, but it seems to be a major job for the goons to accomplish. This is about the most interesting thing going on around here these days. Can you imagine that?

We have a name for the detail I won't mention here, but maybe you have a pretty good guess as to what airmen would call this operation. It doesn't smell very good when it is taking place, but we are glad to have the job done.

August 15, 1944

Several weeks have gone by and nothing unusual has happened, just the same old boring and hungry days. We continue to get one bucket of potatoes daily for each room. This is a one-meal-a-day place. The main topic of discussion is food, food, food. I don't know if it helps or hurts to talk about food when you are hungry. Even if you don't talk about food you are always thinking about something to eat.

I have dreamed about the good food I would choose if I could order what I want to eat. The foods that have not been my favorites, or I just didn't like, sound very good to me now. I can assure you I will take some of the I-don't-like-food at any time, and it will taste like a favorite dessert.

I don't know if the Germans are running low on food or if they don't want us to have much to eat. I have a feeling they are hurting because there are two large armies to feed, one in the east and one in the west.

I wonder who is working the farmland since most of the men are fighting. Probably the women are taking care of that chore as the German women are known to be hard workers. Sooner or later the food will come up short and it will be a real problem for them as well as the POWs.

A Loaf of Bread

August 30, 1944

Would you believe, each room has been given a loaf of bread today! What a thrill to see a loaf of dark German bread. Who in our room will cut the bread in equal parts? I am not going to volunteer for the job.

Someone has finally been chosen to divide the bread in 24 equal parts.

Several days ago we were all given a fork, butter knife, and a spoon along with a bowl. We now have a need for the new utensils. The butter knife will come in handy to cut the bread.

Have you ever cut a loaf of bread into 24 equal parts with 23 hungry men watching? This is quite a task. Here is where it really shows how selfish you get when you are hungry. It won't take much to start a real brawl. If someone thinks he is getting a smaller piece of bread than the next guy, then and there the friendship ends.

A decision is made to draw straws for the piece of bread we will get and everyone agrees with this idea. The longest straw drawn gets the first pick of the 24 slices and the shortest straw gets the last slice of bread. Everyone gets their turn according to the length of the straw. There is no problem finding the straws as we head for our mattresses. This solution to equal bread slices has worked well. The bread is good even though it seems to contain a lot of sawdust. I hope we will get more because it helps the hunger pains.

As time goes by it is hard not to worry about my family. I wonder if they have heard that I am alive and in a POW camp. This must be a very difficult time for them. I have no idea how long it takes to get news to the families telling them their son is a POW. Do they still think I am missing in action? That must really be a throat-lumper and very hard for them to endure while waiting for more news. The thoughts of home are always present.

It is difficult to forget about our five crew members we have not seen since before bail out. I do hope they are well and safe. The three other crew members here, Allen, Hunter and Rulong, do not know any more than I do about the rest of the crew. We will have to assume all of them were able to get out of the plane and are safe.

I haven't seen any of the crew members I knew while flying missions out of England. I am sure there are many other camps in Germany where they could be held prisoner. They could even be in this camp but in another compound.

It seems our loss of planes is running high and it has been running high for some time. This involves many airmen. Most of them are saved by bailing out, but a few are saved by crash landings.

Our camp is a place of many rumors and I don't know where or how they originate, but we hear many bits and pieces of news. There is the possibility the men in our group who understand German are getting information. One rumor going around at this time is we will soon be getting Red Cross packages. I hope this rumor is for real. I have no idea what a Red Cross package contains, but just anything along the food line will be most appreciated.

September 7, 1944

We are a week into the month of September and it has given us more time to get used to this experience. The hardest part is not knowing how long this war will last and how long I will have to be hungry and to endure other problems. It is difficult to be positive about our suffering when each day is a duplicate of the day before. We have no way of knowing what tomorrow will bring except that it will probably be the same as yesterday and the day before . . . day before . . . day before . . . day before . . .

Fighting for Bread

The German guards continue to observe and listen to our conversations during the day as they stroll slowly by and then stop occasionally. They have dogs accompanying them on their rounds. I am sure the goons are very intelligent and are trying to look illiterate. This is another one of the German tricks.

Some of the rooms in our compound have been thoroughly searched. I am thankful our room hasn't been. It is difficult to hide anything personal such as the notes for this story and I surely don't want them to be confiscated. I feel sure the searching is the result of what the goons are hearing from under our floors.

The initial order of business each day is the head count as I described the first morning in camp. We do have problems because the Germans are not good at counting. On several occasions we have had to stand in formation for two hours while the count is done. It is not always the fault of the Germans because our own comrades have been found oversleeping. In this case the counters have to search each room to find the missing POW. You can imagine how angry the rest of us get when this happens. That person is in the doghouse on both sides. When someone is missing, we are called by name and have to yell "Here."

Back to food again. For ten days we have been hearing that our Red Cross parcels are to arrive soon. It is likely just a rumor as no packages have come. We are still on that potato diet each day with a loaf of bread once a week. On several occasions we received two loaves of bread and that helps a little. The bread is brought into the compound on open carts that are usually pulled by a horse. Yesterday one of our roommates managed to snitch a loaf of bread as the cart was parked down at the end of the compound. He just casually walked by and slipped a loaf under his light jacket and came back to our room.

He didn't get caught by the Germans, but he might as well have been caught by them because of what happened when he came back to our room. He was asked if he intended to share this loaf of bread and he said "No." That was the wrong thing for him to say.

The snitcher is from New York and there is a fellow from

Tennessee with a hot temper. They got into a terrible fight right here in our room. We let them fight it out for a while until the guy from Tennessee was getting the best of the bread-snitcher from New York.

Some of us felt the fight must be broken up because if the Germans find out a fight is taking place it means solitary confinement. We do not want this to happen because it will probably mean our room will be under stricter surveillance. We will all be tight-lipped about the altercation.

We have learned a lesson from this experience because we realize how selfish we have become due to our empty stomachs —and the stomach controls the mind.

I have been spending time observing those around me to see how they react to different situations and how they conduct themselves in these situations. The one thing I have noted is that we all act differently under the same circumstances. Many flare up very easily, so I try to avoid disagreements. I feel sorry for some of the POWs who have such a difficult time controlling their tempers. I have found it is much better for your own sake and those around you to be as calm and reserved as possible.

The Red Cross Comes Through

September 14, 1944

This is the third month in captivity and enough time has been spent here to realize how much the small things in life count and how many things are taken for granted. Even a small item like a toothpick can be very important. I now realize I can manage without many of the things I used to think were necessary. Being hungry all of the time is terrible. When this ordeal passes I hope and pray I will never be hungry again during the rest of my life.

There are many more things I have taken for granted. The

freedom to worship God in my own way is very important to me. To live in the United States of America as a free person means more than words can express. I am taking time to count my blessings. I am blessed to have a wonderful family, good friends . . . and the list is endless. This is the time to do a lot of thinking and I am sure most of the men here are doing the same thing.

Today is going to be a happy day for all of us as we have been told the Red Cross parcels are here. I can't get adjusted to an empty stomach and I am not alone. There is just too much talk about food, and the constant hunger pains make it difficult for us to forget about the subject.

It is really true! A large truck has come into the compound and they are unloading boxes of Red Cross parcels. Hopefully they will get them to us before too long. It seems they are distributing them now down at the end of the compound. This will be like getting a special Christmas present.

We still don't know the contents of the parcels, but it won't be long before we can see for ourselves. We have been promised one parcel each, but to our regret that has been cut in half. We will have to share the box with a partner. That won't be as bad as sharing with twenty-four men.

This is a time for self-control and we must not eat everything at once or even in a day or two. We have to be careful to keep from getting ill. Eating too much at one time after a lengthy starvation diet will make one sick. The stomach needs to adjust to eating more food, so stretching it out as far as possible is good advice. We don't know when the next parcel will arrive, but we have been told they will be coming weekly. We cannot depend on that information, so I will spread out the contents of this one as far as I can. Even if we continue to get only the usual potatoes and bread, things will be much better as far as food is concerned.

One of the items included in the parcel is cigarettes. Smokers have been craving a smoke and their need for cigarettes is almost as bad as a craving for food, so I am lucky that I don't

Cigarette packages from the Red Cross gave me writing paper.

smoke. There is a lot of trading going on. This will help me as I can trade my cigarettes for food. The poor smokers are trading their food for cigarettes and depriving their bodies of much-needed nourishment.

We need to set up an exchange system and I am sure we will get this worked out so it will be fair to everyone. It is good to get soap, and the fair exchange system will not be needed for this item. No one will trade soap. We can all use a little cleaning with that product. You can imagine what we look like, and smell like, without soap for body cleansing.

September 28, 1944

As time goes by it is late in September and it is beginning to get cold in this part of Germany. I imagine it can get very cold here in the winter.

We will need to exercise more as it gets colder. There is no controlled exercise program, so each one is on his own to stay in fair physical condition. Of course our energy level is limited due to the shortage of food. I can assure you no one will have an overweight problem while in this POW camp. Our problem is being underweight. I am guessing I have lost about 20 to 25 pounds, but there is no scale for weighing.

Walking in the compound next to the barracks is getting to be my favorite pastime, and it is true for many others. I don't walk fast, but I also do some sit-ups, a few push-ups, arm exercises, and the Air Force hop. We are able to do more exercising now that our diet has improved.

I know it is very important to exercise the body and mind—exercising the body is very good for the mind at a time like this. It erases some of the negative thoughts. Exercising, along with my faith in God, helps make me a more positive person. I never realized it could be so hard to think positive thoughts, but I know it is very important in this situation. We must look at the brighter side of things because, in my heart, I know there is a rainbow somewhere down the road.

When I find the right person to talk to about our present conditions, I am in luck and we can help each other very much. All of a sudden, after a serious discussion with a friend, our ordeal becomes easier to accept.

Midnight Shakedown

October 6, 1944

Days go by and nothing unusual happens in camp, but it is evident something is causing the guards to be very suspicious today. It doesn't take much to get them stirred up. Most of the time the majority of us don't know what is going on, but it is evident something is causing them to be concerned. When this happens it is time to worry and we are all uptight about what they might do.

Minor inspections take place regularly in different rooms. This is done by higher ranking German officers. They appear at the door without prior notice and order everyone out of the building. You cannot return until everything has been thoroughly checked. I hope they never find anything to cause a problem with us. Most of the daytime inspections are not too bad, but what happened in Barracks Two last night was a first in this compound. We were told what happened this morning. Suddenly around midnight all the lights came on in every room in Barracks Two. The lights are controlled by one switch for the entire building. When the lights came on everyone was ordered out immediately and they were not given time to put on extra clothing. A guard came into each room at the same time shouting "Rouse, Rouse", and that means get moving fast. They did not know what was happening but were told to get out of the barracks and get out fast.

It was cold last night, so it was uncomfortable to be outside with very little clothing on their backs. They soon found out this was going to be a complete shakedown. There must have been two dozen troops taking part in the search.

I was told what happened by my friend John. His room is in Barracks Two. The search was not accomplished in just a few minutes—it took almost two hours before they could go back inside.

My friend said you would not believe what they found when they stumbled back into the dark barracks. First of all, they were waiting for the lights to be turned on so they could get back to bed. The lights never did come on after the inspectors left the room. To their horror every straw mattress, or should I say sack, had been dumped of its contents in the middle of the floor. A thorough search had been made and the empty bedsacks were piled in the corner of the room. There was total darkness and John said if there ever was a time to be calm and patient with your roommates, this was it.

Needless to say, it was impossible to divide the straw into twenty-four sacks in total darkness, so all decided to wait for the morning light before starting the task of refilling the mattress sacks.

The beds were not the only problem, because everyone has a few personal items including clothing, and these items were also scrambled. John said this could have developed into a terrible situation among his roommates.

Later today I talked to John again and asked how things worked out on the sorting job. He said, "We all worked together a large part of the day and things turned out very well. Everyone acted like mature men as we put the room back together." Working together was a must in this situation.

We haven't heard if the guards found what they were looking for and we have no idea what caused the search.

I always get prepared for lights out long before the scheduled time because we never know exactly when they will be switched off for the night and it will be total darkness until daylight.

October 16, 1944

It is evident this is the fall of the year because it is getting colder every day. The fall brings back memories of my early childhood. It was not easy for my dad to secure wood for winter heating on the farm in Texas. I am remembering the late twenties and the Model T Ford era. Where we lived was strictly farm country and there was no wood available. Early in the fall of each year a wagon was readied, the wheels greased, and any needed repairs were made for the trip to get firewood.

The load of wood was usually very heavy, so two of the best mules were selected to do the wagon-pulling job on this round trip of about twenty miles. We started early in the morning so we would be back home by evening. The trees had been felled and trimmed of the smaller branches by tree cutters who owned or leased the property. Since the trees were about fifteen feet in length they had to be loaded length-wise on the wagon. It didn't take long to load the trees, but the mules had to have time for a good rest before starting back home with the heavy load.

I remember one time my dad even selected and cut the trees himself. I went with him in our Model T Ford on that trip and then later the wagon trip was made to haul the wood home. The price was better if you cut your own wood and that is the reason my dad did his own cutting.

October 24, 1944

Today our food menu has changed. It is something I would not eat if I were at home. Our story is the same because we are still hungry all of the time, and anything new along the food line gets our attention. The new menu item is a mixture of dehydrated vegetables with the primary ingredient being cabbage, kohlrabi (a turnip-looking cabbage I had never heard of before today), and some carrots. It is like watered-down soup, but it does taste good.

No matter what it tastes like I will eat my share to get something in my stomach. It will fill a little of the empty space and that is good. I would not pick this item on a menu if I had a choice, but this is not a restaurant and I have no choice here. Come to think of it, they wouldn't dare put this item on a menu. I am glad to accept anything that is edible and hope to get enough to sustain me during these trying times.

October 26, 1944

Every day I gain new personal friends; it is difficult to talk about "days gone by" to just anyone. It seems we always end up talking about the awkward situation we are in right now and what we think will happen to us in the future. The future is very uncertain so it is important to remember the good things about our past. We need to remind each other that even under the adverse situation we are in, we still are very lucky to be alive. We must believe this ordeal will end and we will all be able to go home and our dreams will come true.

We are forming what we call an "exchange club." When we get home each person in the club will send their state's favorite food to all of the club members. I will send Texas pecans to everyone. We are also planning menus using the food we will receive from each member. We are only dreaming, but this conversation contains no military secrets, if by chance the Germans are listening to us.

A Surprise

October 31, 1944

Today I have special memories of my mother as this is her birthday. I know she is very concerned about me, her only son. I pray it will not be too long before our family will again be together.

Something good has happened today. We have been given a New Testament pocket-size Bible. For this gift I thank the American Red Cross.

We have had no reading material up to this point and I miss reading very much. Being able to read is something I have always enjoyed. Reading is another thing we take for granted. We all need to read good material to stimulate our mind and this is especially true for us under these circumstances. The New Testament will help the thinking of those of us who plan to read and study this great book. It will also give us something special to do on the long days. I can hardly wait to start reading this new treasure, the Holy Bible.

The Bible brings back memories of my early childhood days in the country Lutheran Church where my family belongs. My parents saw to it that we attended Sunday School every Sunday. We also attended some church services even though my sisters and I were very young.

Church nurseries for children were unheard of then, so the entire family was expected to sit together regardless of age and the children were supposed to be quiet. Mothers seemed to be reluctant to take the young children outside when they began to cry. I can remember, as a young child, how noisy it got with the babies crying and the pastor trying to preach his sermon. At times, the pastor would pause until things got quiet.

The country churches were not air conditioned and it was hot and uncomfortable in the summer. The Sunday School rooms were not as hot because the classes were held an hour earlier. Our Sunday School class was special because of the dedicated and thoughtful teachers who made learning about the Bible very interesting. This was true even for the very young children.

I believe the early start in church participation has given me strength, faith, and courage to face the hard times like I am going through now. I know in my heart these bad times will pass and we will be the victors in this war. I feel we will soon be on our way home.

The Dogfight

November 1, 1944

We are in a very remote area of Germany, and it is unusual to see or hear any type of aircraft or anything to remind us that a war is being fought in this country.

Today a most exciting and unusual incident occurred. At

first we heard what sounded like a fighter plane buzzing high in the sky, then another fighter plane was seen. An Allied fighter and a German fighter were having a dogfight within our sight. It didn't last long, but the winner was the Allied fighter pilot and you should have heard the shouts of joy and jubilation from the POWs.

As you can imagine, the German guards were not too happy about the incident, so we curtailed our joy in front of them because we do not want to irritate the guards.

I can't help but wonder how the two planes ended up in this part of Germany this far from targets. I doubt we will have an answer any time soon—or maybe never. Only the Allied fighter pilot will be able to explain how the dogfight came about in this area.

At least we had something happen today that was more interesting than watching the Germans pump out the latrine!

November 3, 1944

After the excitement of a few days ago, things are back to the same boring routine. But we have our New Testaments to read and for that I am thankful.

We have known for sometime that through the Geneva Convention agreement we, as non-commissioned officers and higher ranks, will not be permitted or forced into any type of labor or work. That is why we are not doing any camp chores. As of this date they have honored that agreement.

November 4, 1944

This is the first week of November, and we haven't received individual Red Cross parcels. We are still having to share with another person and the parcels arrive every two weeks instead of every week. It makes us wonder if the Germans are helping themselves to some of the parcels. I am very thankful for what we are receiving because without this help the food situation would be much worse.

We continue to be counted every morning and the guards still haven't learned how to do it. They have to count over and over many times each morning, and they get very excited if they suspect someone is missing. This means we have to stand in the cold until they are satisfied we are all here. I suppose a report has to be made to the camp commandant each day. The red-headed Gestapo commandant hasn't been seen for some time, so we suspect he has been transferred elsewhere. We didn't see much of him after our first greeting on Day One at the camp. He will not be missed by anyone. I think it would be difficult to find a worse fellow than that officer.

We have received word that some of us are walking too close to the warning wire and the guards will not hesitate to shoot anyone who refuses to obey this order. The guards in the towers at each corner of the compound seem to be very alert and they have their guns ready at all times. I know they mean business and I will not test them.

What About Mail?

About a week after we arrived at camp we were given a post card and a folded sheet of lined paper to write a message to our family. I did not waste any time before starting a letter to my folks. I am wondering if the letter and post card were mailed. The post card had seven lines on the back and we were told to print clearly. I suspect each message will be thoroughly censored and the printing will make it easier for the censor to read.

Later we were given two post cards and two folded sheets to write to our family. As you can guess, I immediately wrote to mine.

Some of the fellows have received mail from home and

this is exciting news for them. The letters have been written on a special type of folded paper. It's designed for sending mail to prisoners of war. They have been censored by the U.S. and the Germans.

I look forward to my first letter. My father is a great writer so I hope it will not be long before his letter arrives.

I will describe the German post card. On the front side there are lines for the name and address of the person the letter is being mailed to and on the lower left side is the *absender* name and POW number. On the top left corner it reads, *Kriegsgef Anenonpost* and *Postkaite*, and on the back, the word *Kriegsfefangenenlager*. There is a place for the *Datum*, which I am sure means the date. The folded paper contains about 25 lines and it is about six inches wide. It is folded and tucked inside the flap. This makes it easier for the censors to open.

I have sent four post cards and four folded letters to date and they have contained the return address we have been told to use. It is important for our families to receive letters from us to assure them we are well. They have been notified of our capture so now their concern is for our well-being in the POW camp.

I can imagine the excitement and joy my family will have when they receive my first letter or card. It is hard to believe how much you can miss your family. This is another adjustment that is not easy to make.

My crew members are also anxiously waiting for mail from home so mail call is something to look forward to each day. It will be a happy day when we all have receive that important letter from home.

November 6, 1944

My first letter from home has arrived! What a great feeling to know my family members are well and they have received mail from me! My first card and letter arrived at home on September 17, and my Dad's letter was written to me on September 18. He didn't waste any time responding. They were as elated to hear from me as I was to hear from them.

Since he is quite a letter writer, every available line was used. I know he will send as many letters as is allowed. He writes the letters because my mother is not a great letter writer. The folded letter from home is custom-made for POWs and it is similar to what we send to our families.

I hope the mail will continue to come, because this is a morale booster. It is like a rainbow in the sky after a summer rain. In the meantime I will write to my family and some of my friends. I hope to hear from some of them in the near future.

Dad mentioned they are sending a package, but there are many restrictions. He is

The wonderful first letter from home

Part Two: Stalag Luft IV 57

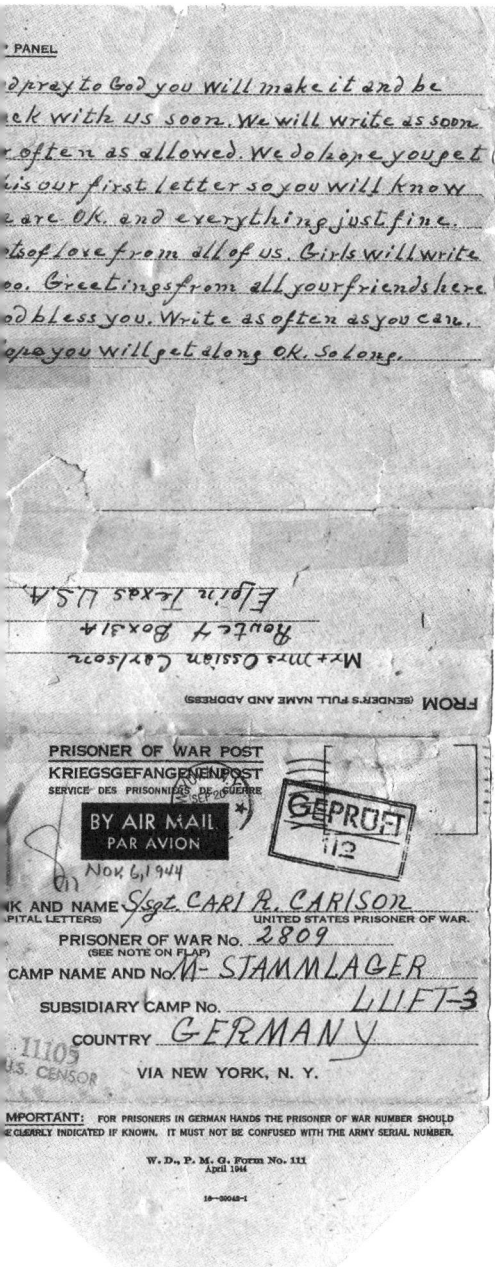

in the process of finding out about the requirements at this time. I have heard of a few POWs receiving parcels from home, but they are few and far between. I feel sure many packages are being sent, but they are just not reaching us, so the question is what is happening to all of the parcels. Are they being opened and kept by the Germans? I do believe the Germans are tempted to keep some of the packages.

The news from home is good, and I know they have heard from me. This makes me feel much better mentally. So for the moment, I have a much better outlook on this whole experience.

Knowing I will receive more mail and my mail is being delivered to my folks is a relief. I had my doubts about the German mail service until my first letter arrived from home. My first letter from Dad is here in my notes. You can tell he used every inch of space to write on the small page.

Athletic Equipment
November 10, 1944

A few items of athletic equipment have been slowly arriving by truck, thanks again to the American Red Cross. This is encouraging to all of us. I have seen a few boxing gloves and these are good for the ones who might want to release some frustration or square off with someone. However, the Germans probably would not know if boxing was for real or not. They might think we were having a true fight. With restricted energy no one is going overboard with any kind of equipment. There are also footballs, baseballs, softballs, and bats. This compound consists of twenty-four hundred men and the space is limited, so the chance of using the equipment is slim.

My parents on the farm

In the meantime I will watch the others use the equipment and continue my exercise by walking. Allen, Hunter, and Rulong walk a lot, so we talk and walk together. Allen and Hunter are married and they both have children.

November 12, 1944

I have met Gus from Austin, Texas. He is in Barracks Number Six and it has been great to get to know him. He happens to be a relative of my sister's boyfriend. We have become real good buddies. I forgot to mention we have received playing cards and Gus is a bridge player.

I don't know anything about bridge, but Gus has insisted I join in a game and he will teach me how to play. I find out very soon that this is a stimulating and interesting card game. I now have become a lousy bridge player. I still have much to learn about the game. It is impossible to play often because the cards are limited and so are the bridge players. Most POWs know a few card games, so the cards have to be shared. Sharing is the name of the game.

A Sunday Sermon

November 14, 1944

As I said, we have Bibles and a few of us are starting a Bible Study Class in the evenings after we are locked in for the night and before lights out.

I have met one POW who was attending Seminary before joining the Armed Forces. He is also from Texas, I might add. I understand he has been negotiating with the Germans to conduct a church service in the assembly building located at the end of the compound.

I now hear he has been successful, so on Sunday we will

have a sermon. The word is spreading fast and we are all looking forward to his first sermon. He is a Protestant, so I don't know if others will come, but I do know they are welcome to join our group. The space will be limited as the room doesn't appear to be very large.

November 18, 1944

Today is my younger sister's nineteenth birthday. I wish I could be at home today and enjoy a cup of coffee and a slice of birthday cake with her. Happy Birthday, Sis!

It is now cold enough to snow and we have had very little sunshine in the past two weeks. I do miss seeing the sunshine. Winter, I believe, will be very cold in this northern area of Germany. I know for sure the weather will be colder than the winters in South Texas.

November 19, 1944

It is Sunday and we are ready to go to Church. There are no seats, so everyone must stand and there are German guards by the dozens. They are everywhere because they seem uneasy during this service. I know they will be listening closely to what our chaplain has to say to all of us today. The guards are stationed around the walls at the front and back of the hall.

We heard a very good sermon and he is a good preacher. In addition, a couple of hymns were sung and it really did sound good. I hope the Sunday Sermon will be allowed to continue. I feel sure it depends on the mood of the German commander.

Christmas in Captivity

December 5, 1944

As time slowly passes, nothing dramatic has happened in

the past several weeks. I still read the Bible each day and we are playing bridge when the cards are available. Of course I try to write notes in my so-called diary when there is a chance to do so, but things are the same each day. We are all hungry most of the time as you well know by now.

My dad has been passing the word around to all of my friends to write. Since each person is limited to the number of times they can write each month, the more people who write the better. I have received a total of seven letters from my parents, sisters, and friends. I am grateful that my parents are making sure I get mail often from my family and friends. Everything I hear from home is on the positive side and I am sure they realize I don't need to hear negative news.

They have to be careful about what they write because of the censors. I also have to be careful of what I write from this side of the fence. We cannot mention anything in our letters about the war. It takes about five weeks to receive my mail and I guess that is not too bad considering mail travels through a war zone.

As Christmas will be here in a few weeks it is difficult to keep from thinking about how it will be observed here in camp. I feel certain we will still be here and this will not be a very happy time. It will probably be a sad, dull, hungry, and gloomy time for all of us. (Now I am being negative, but that is the way I feel.)

I remember, as a child, an important part of Christmas was the hanging of the stockings the night before Christmas, and waking up the next morning and running to see if Santa Claus filled our stocking. The stockings were always filled to the brim, because my mother made sure we had ample surprises.

My father butchered a hog before Christmas and we had smoked sausage, delicious sugar-cured ham, and bacon. Mother started baking weeks before Christmas making cookies, coffee breads, cakes, pastries, and various types of Swedish Christmas breads. The cookies were decorated to look like Santa Claus, stars, and Christmas trees.

Our Christmas tree came from the land where Dad got our heating wood and it was a thrill to go with him and look for the perfect tree. We managed to find that perfect tree every year. My mother and sisters decorated the tree with strings of popcorn, apples, candles, and decorated cookies. The most beautiful sight you will ever see is the small lighted candles, in clip-on holders, glimmering all over the Christmas tree.

When we blew out the candles the house had a wonderful fragrance. To this day, when candles have been blown out it reminds me of my childhood at Christmas.

I cannot figure out how we managed not to set the tree and the house on fire but it never happened, and as far as I know it never happened to any of our neighbors. The Lord was watching over all of us at that memorable time of the year.

Christmas at our country Lutheran Church was special. On Christmas Eve we attended church services. The children were given bags of fruit and candy. Baskets of fruit were passed down the pews of the church and the adults received their special treat of an apple or orange.

Christmas morning we found presents under our tree, as Santa had visited us the night before. You know how children can get excited about presents. Along with my two sisters, Mable and Elizabeth, I spent most of the day looking under the beautiful tree at the mysterious packages. Of course we had dinner with all of the trimmings on Christmas Day.

We always had lutfisk for dinner. Lutfisk is served at Christmas by the Scandinavian people. It is cod fish and it's a Swedish custom to have this special fish at Christmas.

The lutfisk is bought several weeks before Christmas at the local grocery store. Since we live in a Swedish community, the stores carry this delicacy. The dried lutfisk hung in long pieces from the ceiling of the grocery store and it looked like weathered lumber. The odor was not pleasant. Dad would pick the lighter-colored pieces, as that was considered the best choice. It is very dry when it is purchased and it has to be sawed in pieces, about six inches long, and then soaked in lime (wood ashes) water a week to ten days. It was kept in our smokehouse, and cold weather was necessary to keep the fish from spoiling. The smell around the smokehouse was not always pleasant during the preparation time. It was necessary to change the lime water daily. I can remember only a few times that the fish spoiled because of warm weather.

On Christmas Day, the lutfisk is boiled and served in a white sauce with pepper and salt added for seasoning. I loved this Christmas dish along with all of the other goodies. Oh, to have just a little of that good food today!

After our delicious Christmas dinner it was time to open our packages, and the special Christmas gift I wanted was usually under the tree. My parents saw that the children had a good Christmas even though money was in short supply.

During the holiday season it was like an ongoing open house at our home and the homes of our friends. Since we didn't have a telephone our friends would drop by in the evenings or on weekends and no special invitations were needed. Mother kept a supply of goodies and coffee available for our guests. Christmas was always a happy time that I will always remember.

As we grow older we remember that the gifts are not really the most important thing about Christmas. The important thing is being together with our family and friends and attending church services.

This Christmas will be completely different. There will be no family, nothing good to eat, and no special church service.

I do have my POW friends who are in this same situation, so we will celebrate, in a different way, together. We will make the best of the situation and count our blessings even though there is a war going on and we are in a POW camp.

There is so much time for thinking, as you can guess, and my mind does what I call "roaming" from one thought to another. I have both positive and negative thoughts. The very simple things in life are very important.

December 6, 1944

I have been here almost six months and I realize I have not seen a star, the moon, the beautiful evening sky, or the Milky Way. Growing up as a country boy, I would watch the stars almost every evening, and I miss this very much. I also miss hearing the birds sing and seeing a butterfly gently light on a flower.

We take so much in life for granted until it is taken away. Another thing we take for granted is our food, and at times we do not thank the Lord for the blessing of a good meal.

If I come out of this situation alive, I promise to be aware of my blessings and to remember to be grateful for "little things" the rest of my life.

The Sunday gatherings at the assembly hall did not last very long. I have been told that our gatherings will have to take place outside in the cold and rainy weather. They have no consideration for us, even for a church service. We were not given an explanation for the change in location.

December 17, 1944

This is the first Sunday for our outside services and the weather is cold. The guards are again placed around our group assembled to worship, and they seem to be upset and uneasy. Also, the meeting time has been limited to about thirty minutes. I hope we can manage to continue our worship service under these circumstances—at least through the Christmas Season.

December 24, 1944

This is Christmas Eve morning, and it seems like it will be another dreary day here in the POW camp. I feel sure there will be nothing special today. We will probably have the same rations of potatoes, thin soup, and dark bread.

We have had a group of POWs talking to the Germans in charge to see if we can have a little time outside of our barracks on this Christmas Eve. We have now learned the permission has been granted by the camp commandant. We can leave the barracks and go outside for several hours and stay out until midnight tonight. This includes the entire camp of four compounds.

You will not believe how so little given to us can mean so much. It almost seems like a Christmas gift from our enemy.

We have another great surprise on this special day. This morning Red Cross parcels have come in and they are now being distributed to everyone. This will surely be a memorable day and a gift that we will never forget.

We now know this is not the ordinary Red Cross parcel, but a Christmas parcel that contains canned turkey, plum pudding, and other food items especially prepared for our Christmas. What a blessing to receive a gift of food on this special day.

We have so much to be thankful for today, but we must control our eating and not eat all of the food today. Overeating will surely invite trouble with an already weak and hungry stomach. The rich food is especially bad for the empty stomach.

How good this food does taste. This is a real picnic. The Germans realize we have ample food so we do not get the usual bucket of potatoes and the so-called soup and bread for our daily ration. This is one day we do not need their food.

We are now outside on Christmas Eve and I can hear Christmas carols being sung everywhere. Some snowflakes are slowly falling on this cold, windless, and beautiful night. What a sight and sound to behold. Even the German guards seem to listen intently, for after all they are not spending Christmas at their homes either.

Now we have been told we can stay outside until one o'clock. This is really what you call a breath of fresh air. I will never forget this beautiful night.

Now it is time to go back inside and we are given a short time before the lights go out. Someone out there must have a little heart or this would not have happened.

I will not sleep much on this night as there is just too much to think about on this Christmas Eve. Tomorrow—or I should say today—is Christmas Day and I hope it will also be a special day.

Christmas memories are really flooding my mind about when I was growing up on the farm. What really comes to mind is the abundance of food we always had at home. We raised our food and didn't have to buy pork, chicken, or beef products. We had a large garden that produced our vegetables and we also had fruit trees. As you can tell, I am thinking about food, my family, and my home tonight.

December 25, 1944

The Christmas Season at home was a typical Scandinavian

country feast. I would like to be there right now and enjoy all of the festive food and activities. Here I go thinking about food again. We don't have it too bad as I don't believe anyone has been hungry today. We have the Red Cross to thank because they saw to it that the POWs here had a special Christmas that includes enough to eat for two days.

1944–Is It a Year to Remember or to Forget?

I know that I must tolerate the situation here in camp, but it is very difficult to do so on special days such as Christmas and New Years. It is very tough on the holidays of our country such as Independence Day, Thanksgiving, Memorial Day, and so on. At least Christmas and New Years are celebrated by the Germans; thus they are more understanding on these days.

The year 1944 will soon end; it will surely be a year that I will always remember because it will be very difficult to forget. It has been the most arduous time in the twenty-two years of my life. I remember what someone told me and I will try to tell myself, "These times shall pass." This strong message means so much to me today.

As life and time goes on, you really begin to notice the routine of things here and it gets so boring after a while. There is nothing to look forward to because we are merely existing.

At least the new year of 1945 will be here soon and I hope for better things to come in the new year. Everything is so uncertain and I keep thinking that the time spent here is just plain wasted. A part of my life is wasting away. Life is short enough without having to be inactive for any period of time.

December 31, 1944

This is New Years Eve of 1944, it is after 6 P.M., and we have been secured in our barracks as usual. There is an unusual amount of talking which indicates this is a special time for all of us here in camp.

There will be no firecrackers or Roman candles to hear and see on this evening. New Years Eve was one of the highlights of the year in my younger days. Fireworks were a common thing on New Years Eve and also on New Years Day. We really did celebrate the arrival of the new year. Many of us will stay up late to welcome the New Year of 1945.

There is much reminiscing going on. I hear all kinds of stories and experiences from my fellow Kriegies that have taken place on New Years Eve. It almost gives me the feeling and excitement of a new beginning as the old year is gone and the new one has arrived.

It is uplifting to have the chance to read in the New Testament we received some time ago. During the holiday season, it has been very inspiring to read the Christmas Story. The gift of the New Testament means more to me than you will ever know. When I am really down, reading the word of God gives me hope and encouragement.

Part Three
The New Year

January 1, 1945

    Usually as a New Year begins, under normal circumstances there is a bit of excitement felt by most people. New Years resolutions are made by many. Some resolutions are kept and some are not kept, but I haven't given much thought to making a resolution for 1945. I would rather pray that something good will happen this new year such as the end of the war and our country being the victors. Then we can all go home.

    I feel that without a doubt we will win the war, but the real question is just when this will happen. At this stage I doubt that anyone really knows the answer.

    Because I am confident my diary will not be found, it is time to mention some information we have been receiving for the past two to three months. We have been having what we call a news report. The news bulletins are verbal war news reports coming into our compound. I have no way of knowing how these are getting through or who is involved or if it is leaked by the Germans. Maybe there is a radio somewhere in the compound that is hidden by a POW. It is a mystery to me, but a very welcome mystery. Maybe that is why Barracks Two had a total shakedown. As you can tell, it is most important for us to keep very quiet at night as this is the only time the news can be passed along. The news reports go from room to room.

January 11, 1945

Today the word is going around that this camp is to be evacuated because the Russians are coming. This is very good news to all of us here in camp. We know the war is not going well for the Germans.

If we are evacuated, how will the Germans move almost ten thousand POWs and where will we be going? This raises many questions among us. In a way, the thought scares me because we are not as secure when being transported and this makes the Germans jumpy.

I know the guards will not hesitate to shoot if anyone attempts to escape. They will need hundreds of guards if we move and they will probably have guard dogs. Maybe this is just a rumor. I certainly don't mind leaving this camp, but the next camp could be worse.

This is January and the weather is not in our favor. It is very cold and there is snow in many parts of Germany this time of the year. Moving now seems like a bad choice, but if the information is true it means the Germans do not want the Russians to liberate this large POW camp.

Good-bye Stalag Luft IV

January 15, 1945

It is true that this compound will be evacuated on January 30, and that gives us fifteen days to talk to one another about the move. We do not have answers to many questions. Will we ever see each other again after our move from this camp? Will we all go in the same direction? It seems impossible, as I see it, for all of us to go in the same direction. How will we be traveling in this cold weather? Many questions are being asked and we have no answers.

So the Russians are coming and this is no longer a rumor! I hope the Russians will advance so fast that on "moving day" it will be too late for us to be transported out of this camp. In two weeks we will know our fate. One thing I know for sure, it won't take me long to pack and there will be no luggage to worry about.

We will leave here the way we came, with only the clothes on our backs. I hope the shakedown will not be too thorough when we leave because I do not want my diary to be found. My story will go out the window, and I may go with it if it is found in my possession.

January 22, 1945

We have had a week to talk about the impending move. Today we were informed we will be divided into two groups. One group will leave on foot and another group will be transported by rail boxcar. Everyone who is healthy and has no injuries will leave by foot. The rest will get a free ride in a boxcar. Since I have the ankle injury I have been told to "boxcar it." It seems that riding is the better choice, but I didn't have the opportunity to choose the mode of transportation. We must follow orders and hope for the best. I think there will be small groups in each category for easier control by the guards. We may be going in different directions.

I now know that my crew members Allen, Hunter, and Rulong will be walking. Here is where we will part and this is a bit hard to accept because we are close friends. My good friend and bridge instructor from Austin will ride in the boxcars. I don't know if I will see my crew members or my Austin friend again. We do not know if we will end up at the same place when this move is completed. I may never see my roommates or my walking buddies again and I am feeling very sad. Only time will tell what will happen to all of us. I can imagine how much preparation it will take to move this entire camp. It will also require many German soldiers and guards to be in charge of the operation regardless of how we are moved. This is making all of us edgy.

Now we have heard that some groups are leaving on foot from the other compounds and this probably means the walkers will be the first to go. This is what you call breaking up camp. Everything is so uncertain and not knowing what is to happen is very upsetting.

It is now evident that all who have been ordered to walk are in fact the first to leave and they have been told to be ready to go at a moment's notice. It is not too early to wish each other good luck as we will be going our separate ways soon.

I have told my crew members and the rest of my friends good-bye, and we have prayed that God will continue to watch over us in the days ahead.

January 23, 1945

Today the walkers are beginning to leave our compound and that includes my buddies in this room. With over one half of my buddies gone, it seems rather empty. It gives me the feeling that I want to leave also as there is nothing much left here.

Leave, we will, in a day or so. Again many questions come to mind. Who will feed all of us? There appears to be a severe food shortage. How long will this trip last? Where will this all end? Will we be riding in a boxcar and will we be subjected to bombing raids? What about the simple necessary items like drinking water and food? Will we have sanitary facilities on the train? The questions in my mind are going wild.

The Russians Are Coming And We Are Going

January 30, 1945

The rumor we heard two weeks ago is true—we are moving out today. The boxcars are ready for us and we are leaving in the same sloppy formation exactly like when we arrived at this camp. It really gives me a peculiar feeling to leave through these gates, the gates I entered as a Kriegie many months ago. One thing for sure: It feels better with my back to the gates than it felt facing them seven months ago.

I am experiencing a strange sensation, like a light touch of freedom. I can almost feel free as we march away from the camp. Coming back to my senses, I know I am still a prisoner and there are guards with loaded guns and bayonets surrounding our group. It is quite evident we are not free, but it was a good feeling while it lasted.

We are now being loaded into trucks and are beginning to slowly move. No one is waving good-bye to our POW home of seven months. Our stay at this camp will not be remembered with pleasant thoughts. We will remember the hunger pains, being cold, the crowded barracks, being covered with lice, the morning count fiasco, and the German guards. The memories of Stalag Luft IV will remain with me for as long as I live. I am very thankful that I survived my stay in this camp.

The trucks are now stopping and we can see the train. We will be traveling in boxcars as expected. There is a sliding door on one side and a rectangular window on each side of the car. The windows have steel bars and you can tell immediately that this will not be a sightseeing trip.

As we enter the boxcar I realize there are no seats. We will have to rotate between sitting on the floor and standing, as we are very crowded. It is standing or sitting room only. This is a packed boxcar full of unhappy POWs and I have never heard so much grumbling. I can definitely tell that this is going to be an unpleasant and uncomfortable trip.

I have found one good thing to point out about this predicament: There are no guards in this car. It wouldn't be safe for guards to be crowded together with all of us because tempers might flare and cause very serious problems.

I can tell you now that I would gladly trade this boxcar for the car we traveled in coming to Stalag Luft IV seven months ago. I thought that one was uncomfortable, but this is like transporting animals to the slaughter house. If the trip is a short run it won't be too bad, but if we have to stay in this crowded condition for several days we will have a ghastly situation.

The train is in no hurry to leave as we have been waiting here for several hours. I suppose they are loading other cars, so the whole operation will take time. They are doing what seemed to me to be an almost impossible task of moving all of the POWs out of the camp.

No consideration has been given for the comfort of the POWs. We have two buckets here in the boxcar to use when we need to urinate, but I don't know about the "other" at this point. No one will want to be next to the bucket, but there is no way to keep from being fairly close to this makeshift toilet. This is another situation that could make tempers flare, but let's hope for the best.

Since this is winter time and it is very cold, being crowded will help keep us warm. If it were hot outside it would not be tolerable. I can see guards walking slowly up and down beside the boxcars as I look through the window. Guns are slung over their shoulders and cap flaps are down over their ears to keep them warm. I can tell it is windy and I know they must be cold. We are out of the wind, but we are not out of the cold. These cars were built for hauling animals and not human beings.

The Test of Tolerance

This will be a real test of tolerance for all of us. One release that we have is that we can bitch and complain among ourselves all we want to because we cannot be heard by the guards. We can't even be seen by the guards unless they look through the windows located on each side of the car. The two windows are approximately three feet by eighteen inches and that is not very large for an average size boxcar. After close examination, this one seems smaller than the boxcars we have at home.

It is impossible to count the number of POWs in the car, but I would estimate between 50 and 60 of us are crowded together in this small area. There must be many other cars packed like this one, and probably other trains just as loaded. Moving 10,000 men is not an easy job, but I must remember that some are walking and I don't know that number.

January 31, 1945

One day has passed and the train has moved off and on, but most of the time we have been standing still. They did make two stops for us to use an open field bathroom. It was really good to get out of the car, but it wasn't always possible to perform on the spur of the moment in an open field with guards stationed all around. This was about a ten-minute break and now back to the filthy boxcar.

This is a slow moving train, almost as if we are not going anywhere. It moves a few miles a day and the rest of the time we are just parked, but some train switching is going on.

Needless to say some of us in here are getting very restless; one POW was beating on the wall today and he had to be restrained. He finally did calm down with the help of his fellow POWs.

We are always thirsty as we have received very little water. Thank goodness it is winter and one does not need as much water to survive in this cold weather.

February 3, 1945

Today we have been given some bread and boiled potatoes. I would love to have some hot soup like my mother used to make in winter. Soup was on the menu often during the winter at home. Good hot soup and homemade bread would be a delight. Here I go dreaming again.

This uncomfortable crowded situation is almost as bad as being hungry all the time. We are just packed together like sardines. The floor gets hard pretty fast when it is your turn to sit down, and very little sleep is possible.

This is Day Four and we have been parked most of the day in a rather large railroad yard. It is hard to determine if this is a possible target, but it is a busy yard because there is a lot of activity going on all around us. What town are we in at this time? Where we are located is a mystery to me and they are certainly not going to tell us anything.

Some planes were heard today. They were not very close, but close enough for me to know there is air action going on somewhere around this area. I again hope this yard is not a prime target. We have enough problems being cooped up in this miserable boxcar without having to worry about an air raid.

February 4, 1945

This is Day Five and we have left whatever town we were parked in and we have moved slowly for a few hours. We stop for a while and then move for a while. We are now parked in the country on a side track, so we should not be in danger of a bombing raid out here in the countryside. This is something to be thankful for, but it is a little difficult to count your blessings in this situation.

I can see a lot of snow on the ground through our small window. Some guards are near the train and some are in the distance to get an overall view of the train. One of my friends finally got the attention of a guard and began begging for some snow to satisfy his thirst. We didn't know what snow was in German, but we know that water is "vasser", so he began asking for "vasser", then saying snow, but the guard either didn't know what was going on or he was playing dumb. Needless to say no snow was given to my begging friend.

Later on we were let out of the train for our now famous toilet break, and we found that the snow was about a foot deep. You guessed it—we had snow to eat. When we have our breaks it is always in a clear area about two hundred yards from the wooded land. This gives the guards a perfect view in the event someone attempts to escape.

This is also bucket-dumping time as we do this each time we have the toilet break. We take turns doing this chore. As I think about the conditions we are living in here in this boxcar it reminds me of cattle being transported to market. I hope we all make it through this ordeal without getting ill.

February 5, 1945

Day Six and Day Seven have gone by and our trip is still not over. Some of us are wondering if we will ever get off of this train. Do they know where we are supposed to go?

The days have been long, but the nights are really long and it is dark for so many hours. We have no heat, no lights, and we are hungry and thirsty. We are all acting like enemies to each other. It is no easy task to be friendly and you don't even want to see the faces of your close friends. This is not a good situation for any human being to have to endure.

Again I must do some thinking and realize we must tolerate each other and keep our faith and know that things will be better soon. No one dreamed that this trip would last a week and it hasn't ended yet.

I have been thinking of my friends who are walking while we are riding in this boxcar and I am wondering if it is worse than riding. I wonder if we will ever know how the walkers are surviving their march in this cold weather. Maybe someday we will know about their journey.

My main concern has to be the circumstances that I am in at this time. Maybe it is being selfish, but this situation is causing me to feel very selfish.

Arriving at Stalag Luft I

February 7, 1945

This is Day Eight and the train is moving much faster than at any other time since the trip started. It gives me the feeling that someone now knows where we are going and I hope the next stop will be the end of this miserable ride.

I am now thinking about what is in store for us when we finally reach our destination. It surely must be an improvement over this boxcar. This has to be what I would have thought an impossible situation to tolerate. So far, all of us in the boxcar have survived, even though we are hungry, dirty, and a little more selfish. I hope things will change for the better and we will become a little more compassionate towards our fellow POWs. It will be a relief to see some other faces when this journey comes to an end.

We are now entering another city and the train is slowing down to a crawl but it has not stopped. We keep hoping that at the next stop orders will be given for the last time to get off of the train and stay off for good.

We are stopping. After eight long days it appears that we have arrived at our final destination. The past eight days will surely be the longest eight days of any time in my life and I hope never to go through anything like this again.

Someone did see a sign out of the small window that said that we are in Barth, Germany. I don't know that much about Germany as I have never heard of Barth. I do know that it was not one of our military targets for the Air Force while I was flying.

It is now official and the trucks are ready to haul us somewhere. We will have to take our turn as it appears that our number is very large.

It will take time to transport all of us to the new camp. Maybe some of our group will be able to walk if given the opportunity. Walking feels so odd after not walking for over a week. I realize that my physical condition must be pretty bad as I try to walk after that miserable train ride.

Everyone is very quiet as that is the rule when the guards are around us. Keeping a low profile is important to remember as we could be in trouble if we cause any problems. I can see that there are more people living in this part of Germany. It is more densely populated around this area than it was near Stalag Luft IV. The German civilians do not seem to mind having American POWs close by. I imagine they have seen many POWs, by the way they act.

We have been ordered by the guards not to bother the German people and I now see that the guards are waving their arms so as to shoo the people away from us.

The trucks did not accommodate many of us, so we are beginning to walk again in our famous sloppy formation. It seems that we are walking through the middle of this town. Many people are standing on the sidewalk watching us go by. I can just imagine what they are thinking: "What a good job the German Army is doing by capturing so many of the enemy soldiers." For that matter, it really does look that way and that is frightening.

We are now leaving the city and walking on a highway that leads out into the countryside. Word has gotten around that this walk will be a little over two miles and our new camp is called Stalag Luft I. How the word gets around is beyond my comprehension.

Our New Home — Stalag Luft I

As we arrive at our new home we find out that this is an officers' camp, or it has been until we arrived. This is where our pilots, co-pilots, and navigators are being confined. Maybe by some remote chance my pilot, co-pilot, and navigator will be here.

Our group of non-commissioned officers will probably

have their own compound and the group will be divided as it was in Stalag Luft IV.

Entering the camp I find that it is not much different from the other one. The gates, guard towers, high barbwire fences with warning wires, and the buildings look almost identical to Stalag Luft IV, but these buildings are obviously older.

I hope the first items on the agenda will be a hot shower and in some way washing our clothes. I have never felt so filthy. I am always hungry and I am anxious to see what they will have for us to eat. With this many new POWs coming in it is no telling what rations we will have, if any. Most likely the old-timers will have to share what they have been getting to eat with the newcomers. Our arrival is bad news for them and for us if that is true.

We did have a shakedown, but not as thorough as some we have had in the past. This is almost a repeat performance of the last camp. I will be in Barracks 303, Room 1-D. It looks like this will be a place to make new friends as none of my friends from the other camp are in this room. I hope some of my friends from the boxcar will be assigned to this room as we got to know each other very well. I suppose it does not matter who is assigned where, as we are just glad to get off that train.

Surely things will settle down and get back to the usual boring and hungry routine again. I just hope that we won't be subjected to the guards watching us every minute. That in itself is very strenuous and quite frightening, especially if they are upset. Sometimes they are given insane orders by their superiors and we are the scapegoats.

Everyone is hoping for better food here since this is an officers' camp, but the word is out that it is not much better and they serve about the same small amount of food. That is not good news.

One improvement here is the latrine building. At least it is enclosed, thus making it much more decent than Stalag Luft IV. A washroom and a few showers are also part of this building, but there is no warm water for washing or showering. Cold water is better than no water at all—we are grateful for any kind.

Our clothes do not dry fast after washing in this area. I found this out quickly when I first washed my clothing.

I have been informed that we are less than a couple of miles from the coastline of the Baltic Sea. That means we are not very far from Sweden and Norway. Since I have relatives in Sweden, it would be nice to be able to escape to that country. Oh well, I am just dreaming.

The living conditions are just as crowded here, as we have twenty-four men in each small cramped room. We have the same slats on our beds with straw sacks for a mattress. Can you believe that the beds do feel good after the boxcar ride? I keep telling myself that things could be much worse. The way for me to keep going is to look forward to the end of the war and the end to these living conditions.

The food has been very sparse with thin soup that contains potatoes and dehydrated vegetables. There is not as much griping about the food here as there was back at our base in England. We wish we could trade for what was served there as we now realize it was very good. We even had a choice of how we wanted our eggs prepared on base before going on a mission. Occasionally they did run out of eggs and then they offered powdered ones. Of course, this was not very popular and did not compare with the fresh eggs. One dish that they prepared for lunch or dinner was called "sh— on the shingle."

I thought it was pretty good, but it caused a lot of griping and grumbling among our group. It is also known as "hoof on the shingle." This was creamed ground meat served on toast. It was served in the mess halls quite often. Mother didn't make anything like that back home on the farm when I was growing up. This was a new dish to me that was served often in the mess hall.

Here I am getting carried away on food again and it seems that the stomach has a way of controlling your mind.

It has been an ordeal just to get your chance to clean up around here. Can you imagine several hundred of us coming into camp at the same time? The few facilities have been very crowded and it is impossible to accommodate everyone quickly. I don't know which is the most important—to clean yourself or get your clothes washed. Cleaning yourself without washing your clothes does not help very much. Since no cleaning has been done to my body or my clothes for a couple of weeks I am very dirty and smelly.

The odor in the boxcar was getting pretty bad, so breathing this fresh air is something I am very thankful for. This is another time that I think about little things of life we usually take for granted. You will never know how much this fresh air means to me.

My chance has finally come to clean up and how good that makes me feel. My clothes are sort of half clean, but at least they feel fresh. We do have two sets of underwear, so at least I have something to wear while my other set is drying. We hang our clothes right here on the bed to dry, and being on our bed means there is less chance of their being lost.

We do have some used razor blades for shaving, so that task is possible to accomplish, but we only have cold water and regular bar soap. We also use the same bar soap for washing our hair. I do not wash my hair often because of the damp cold climate.

It is a little difficult to find a place of silence where I can just sit and meditate by myself for a few minutes. Even at night when the lights are out there are those who have to keep talking until I fall asleep. There is also some snoring and I can pray as I lie awake listening to the snoring.

Thoughts often come back to June 6 of last year, D-Day, and how it was kept a secret, and how shocked and surprised we all were at the morning briefing when we found out this was going to take place. We had been told to hit the sack early in preparation for the next bombing mission and this was not the first time we had been told to do so. Usually we got up around 4:00 A.M. so we would have ample time for all the details, but this next mission somehow appeared unusual because we had just gotten to sleep when we were awakened at 11:00 P.M. and told to get up and go to breakfast and then on to the briefing room. Our breakfast was the usual fresh eggs, bacon, toast, coffee, juice, etc. There was more than the usual amount of grumpiness that morning. A little after midnight everyone wanted to know what in the world was going on and what could be so important or so critical that we had to start this mission so early. We were told that we would find out at the briefing and we certainly should not be late for this different and unusual briefing.

When you entered the room, with the large covered maps up front with the red line showing the target for the mission, you held your breath hoping for a short line that meant a short bombing run. The long lines were there just as often as the short lines.

On this early morning of June 6, 1944, we were amazed to see rather short lines. We had expected that this was going to be the longest mission of our tour. We still did not know what was happening on this historic day. We were all seated and then we were informed that this was the invasion day and that we were scheduled to bomb the coast of France in support of our ground forces.

Of course, more time was spent in preparation for this mission than the actual time involved flying there and back. We were flying over England for at least three hours just grouping with other squadrons. This operation involved thousands of bombers and the sky was thick with planes like masses of flying birds. I surely admired the pilots and navigators for being such experts at a time when just a very small error could have been a quick disaster for a crew.

After briefing, everyone was given the opportunity to go to chapel for a word of prayer with the chaplain. He prayed that this would be a safe mission and he had additional prayers that gave me comfort. I always took the time to go to chapel as I believed that this special prayer time gave me the extra strength needed to do my job on dangerous missions. Not everyone went to chapel this day, but I would guess that one in four did.

As we rolled down the runway with a full bomb load and maximum fuel in the tanks, I always prayed that the B-17 would somehow get off of the ground. Once we were off the ground the plane usually stayed up and this was to the credit of our good pilots. As we ascended into the air we could rest at ease until we were told by the pilot to fire all guns for testing. What happened over enemy territory was a different story on each bombing mission—none were the same.

At least I have had some quiet time this night and time to think. I keep wondering what happened to our other crew members. I haven't found out if they are in this camp. This keeps entering my mind and it is not easy to erase. This is another thing that I think about when I have some quiet time. I have talked to many POWs here and it seems that the chances of all crew members making it to safety is very slim.

Now my thoughts are back to the invasion day mission. This mission was number nineteen for me. Some of the crew members missed missions on occasion for various reasons such as illness or other duties. The missing member was always covered by a replacement as no position was left vacant. Because of D-Day we surely anticipated a tough mission, but to our surprise and delight we encountered no resistance of any kind. There was no flak or enemy fighters. I suppose our numbers were far too great on this day for the German fighter planes to attack. We also had our fighter planes on the prowl looking for action. This turned out to be an easy mission.

Of course, the time spent in preparation and our lack of sleep was not comfortable. We took off at 3:30 A.M. and we were back at our base at 11:00 A.M., this making a total time of seven and one-half hours. As I have said, most of this time was spent organizing and waiting for our turn to hit the French coast.

Now I am thinking again about other flights as well as D-Day. It is always back to the briefing room after every mission and we are questioned and make a report on anything unusual that we have observed. We had to report flak positions, enemy fighters, number of planes going down including our planes as well as the enemy planes. We also reported anyone in trouble, parachutes seen after planes were shot down. Thus, our reports were very important and valuable for future flights. The after-flight briefings took about thirty minutes.

Now I am thinking about the ground crews. They must have been the best ever as they kept our planes flying and we did not have mechanical failures very often. It is easy to forget what an important part they played in keeping the planes in the air. We all trusted and depended on them to do their job well. They deserve a resounding vote of thanks. At times I would wonder how our planes could keep going and going, but I am sure it was due to the excellent upkeep and superior crew chiefs and mechanics. Thinking back on this tonight is like a dream, but I am awake, not asleep.

This ordeal seems kind of like a waiting game, something we can tolerate if it doesn't go on forever. As I have mentioned before, the worst thing about this whole affair is the unknown. At least people that are sent to prison know how long their stay will be, but this is not our case. We do not know the date of our release and there is no getting out early for good behavior. If good behavior would get us out early this place would no doubt be empty in a very short time.

Time is going so slowly and it is near the end of February 1945. It really hurts that I can't be out there helping my buddies win this war. At least we are probably a little burden on the Germans as we are keeping a few men from being on the front lines or in the air. We have to believe that this will help in some small way.

Things would be a little better if I could get some more mail from home, but because of the move it will surely be delayed. I just hope some mail comes through soon.

One never knows what will come up next around here. I have been scratching and itching here and there much more than normal. I have just examined my tee shirt and it is full of lice eggs. It has to be lice eggs as I can see the adults crawling around and that is what has been itching. So off with the shirt as I take it to the wash room for a good scrubbing. After hanging the shirt in the sun to dry all I can see is many more lice, so back for another wash job. I have now included my body and my hair in the wash job. This is a very itchy problem that has developed. I have found out that others are having the same itchy problem, so I will just have to keep fighting the lice the best way possible.

The latest report from our secret source of news is encouraging. There are still some trouble spots, but generally the news is better. Possible the BBC is getting news to someone here in our camp. I hope and pray that the good news is true, but I do believe in my heart that we are getting correct information. What we are hearing is that in spite of all of the air losses we have suffered, our Air Force is getting stronger and this is why we are winning the war over the Germans. The target areas are getting smaller and our losses are down. All of this encouraging information makes it a mite easier to tolerate this terrible situation here in POW camp.

We have several ace fighter pilots here in camp who are high ranking officers and they have been given access to the compounds where we are located. Since they are officers they can discuss our problems with the Germans and this is somewhat encouraging.

The rest of us are like dirt under the Germans feet, but we don't mind as long as we are not bothered too much. If the Germans leave us alone and do not hassle us I feel somewhat safe from the grips of the enemy.

It is enough to see the Germans of higher rank every morning when we have to line up and be counted. I suppose the morning counting fiasco will go on for as long as we are here. It is still nerve-racking to say the least and it does seem like I would get used to this procedure, but I can't really say that it gets any easier. Everything is so uncertain and I can never tell what else they might be up to, especially if things don't please them. They might just simply decide they don't like Americans or English people.

Thinking about liking people, the Bible says to love your enemy. It is odd how difficult this is to abide by because if you really loved your enemy, how could you shoot to kill one another? This is one question I hope to have answered some day.

Those of us who came by boxcar have been here for almost a month now, and it should be enough time to get fully used to this place. The procedures are not that much different from the other camp and we did not come here expecting any im-provements in respect to food and conditions.

First Mail at Stalag Luft I

Some of our group are beginning to receive mail for the first time since we arrived. The mail has our first camp's address without any forwarding address. I guess someone knows where we are located. I just wonder how they are getting the mail to the walkers. It appears that they have records showing where each person is located. I am surprised that they can keep track of everyone as that in itself is not an easy task. I wonder what their motive is for keeping track of everyone as we are just nothing but a number anyway.

If the Germans keep accurate records on each POW, then maybe we will be getting mail from home soon. The last letter I received was on January 28, 1945. That was two days before we left Stalag Luft IV. At that time I was receiving mail about every two weeks.

Now let's go back to this lice problem. After they were discovered on my body my imagination goes wild with the thoughts of those devils being everywhere. Everywhere includes my straw bed, and when you are trying to sleep you can feel them crawling whether they are there or not. This is a very uncomfortable and aggravating situation as there is nothing that you can do to correct the problem. This is just another added condition to suffer through and to make life even more miserable.

March 4, 1945

The first letter I have received at this camp arrived today. This special letter was postmarked December 15, 1944. It was addressed to the Stalag Luft IV address and the envelope shows no forwarding address. It is from my father and he has carefully printed the words very small, but clear. There is such a limited area for writing that he has to make use of every inch of space. It is amazing how much information he can put on such a small sheet of paper.

Elgin, Texas
Dec. 12, 1944

> Dearest Son: Here we are again with a few lines. We wonder how you are getting along. We had a card and a letter from you two weeks ago and they were written August 3, 1944 and August 9, 1944. It sure takes mail a long time to get here, but we are awfully glad to hear from you once in a while. We do hope you have received some of our mail now. We are all well and everything is just fine here at home. Please don't worry about us. We finally got a cold, dry norther, so today we butchered two hogs. Oscar came late, so Ocie and I were just about through with the first hog when he got here. Sold one half and took some to be cured. Elizabeth is coming home tomorrow for a couple of days and Mable was home last Sunday. Carl has been home for a few days, but has left for some place in the military. He is a fine boy. Would sure be swell if I could drop you one of those long letters. I think I could easily break the record now if I could turn the pen loose, and we have a feeling that you could also if you were in a position to do so.

However, we are very glad indeed to get what we get from you and you try to take the best possible care of yourself. Hope this mess will be over soon. Hope to hear from you real soon again. Greetings from all of our friends. Lots of love from us all here and God Bless You.

Mother & Dad

It is such a relief to know that things are well and good with my family. That is one worry that I can lay aside. I guess it is harder on them than it is on me as I know that I am all right. I feel sure that they worry quite a lot and I can surely understand that it must be very hard on them. The letters that I have received will always be a treasure to me and I feel sure that I will never forget how important they have been to me here in this POW camp.

It is the same old usual boring grind around here. I have been looking at the barbwire fences that surround the camp. How sad it is that human beings are actually being fenced in by barbwire. As I grew up I thought there was only one use for this wire and that was to keep cattle, horses, and mules in their proper pasture. Growing up on a farm there were always fences to build and repair. The animals thought that the grass was greener on the other side of the fence, like we hear so often. Many times they would just lean on the fence and it would break or a post would come loose. Often our fences would cross a creek that was dry most of the time, but a big rain would come and wash out the gap. This meant emergency repair time to keep our animals from getting into the wrong pasture or on the road. This is one thing that had to be done on Sunday if the rains came on Saturday.

When I was young I couldn't be of much help on the farm, but I was expected to do what I could as every bit of help was needed. We all had chores assigned to us and we were responsible for their completion in good order.

Here the barbwire fences are not built like the ones on our farm. It is a different ball game keeping human beings fenced in than it is for animals. Not even a goat could get through the fences here as the wires are very high and slanted at least two to three feet towards the inside at the top. These fences are stretched very tight with long barbs close to each other.

About ten feet from the barbwire fence is a single wire that is electrically charged, and there are guards in the towers above the fences at all times. This makes any thought of trying to escape an impossible dream. It would be committing suicide to try to escape from this POW camp.

We are in a waiting game just hoping for good news. It would be nice if we had someone here to tell us, "cheer up, things will get better," but all of the positive thinking has to come from within each of us and this makes it very hard to bear. I keep hearing more doom and gloom than anything else around here. Once in a while I do find a friend that looks at the brighter side of things and then together we realize that things could be worse than they are at this time.

I am thinking of a song that we used to sing, "Count your many blessings, name them one by one, count your many blessings, see what God has done." I have decided to spend some time just counting my blessings. I am alive. I am not ill. I have received letters from my family and they are fine. I am an American. I am a Christian.

It is now the early part of March 1945 and the food problem isn't any better, but we have received a couple of Red Cross parcels to share. My cigarettes again have been traded for something to eat. I realize that I have another blessing to count and this is that I do not smoke. I am much better off than the smokers as they will sacrifice food for cigarettes. Smoking must be a tough habit, to prefer a cigarette over food when you are very hungry. Since I have never been a victim of tobacco, there is no way to really know the smokers' situation without walking in their shoes.

There is only one thing that I want from the cigarettes and that is the container or the wrapper. I am using the blank part of the wrapper to record my diary. I have had no problem in getting the cigarette papers and for this I am thankful. I am writing very small and it is amazing how much I can write on this paper. I can also hide my diary much easier since it is small. I usually secure it in the straw of my bed. The beds are seldom searched, so I figure that this is a safe place for my precious diary. I have made a small booklet using cigarette package covers for the pages, and cardboard for the cover, and some string to hold everything together. The brands of cigarettes sent to us by the Red Cross are Raleigh, Old Gold, Camel, and Chesterfield. I have a feeling that these cigarettes are being donated to the Red Cross by the cigarette companies. On the Old Gold wrapper it reads, "The Treasure of Them All", and on the Camel wrapper it reads, "Choice Quality." There are no comments on the other two brands. I think that someday it will be discovered that cigarette smoke is not good for the lungs. As far as the future is concerned, if I ever get out of here, I will surely remember how people can get hooked on tobacco. Maybe this is one good lesson that I have learned while being in this POW camp.

Another important lesson is to be grateful for the small things in life and for life itself. Many thoughts come to my mind as this is one thing that I can do here—think. Sometimes I begin to think that I am running out of good and normal thoughts and when that happens it is not a good feeling. When I get this way I find a good friend to talk with.

It does help to talk about our problems as things do brighten up for both of us when we can talk about our situation.

At times when I get despondent I find that I am missing my special crew buddy, Allen. I have seen that he has strong faith and this is really the kind of person that is of great help when I need to talk. I think of Allen and wonder where he is at this time. Is he still walking with the group that left the first camp, or did he go to a different camp? Maybe some day we will see each other again.

This is Sunday, March 4, 1945, and I am giving you a look at our menu. We had one sixth of a small loaf of bread, and one cup of very thin soup without seasoning. This is our meal for the day.

It has been a long time since we received a Red Cross package, so the word "hungry" is heard very often around here. Added to being hungry all of the time, the weather is miserable. It is cold and wet.

I attended our church service today and it was indoors and closely watched by the German guards who understand English. It must be very hard for our chaplain to prepare the sermon in a place like this with each

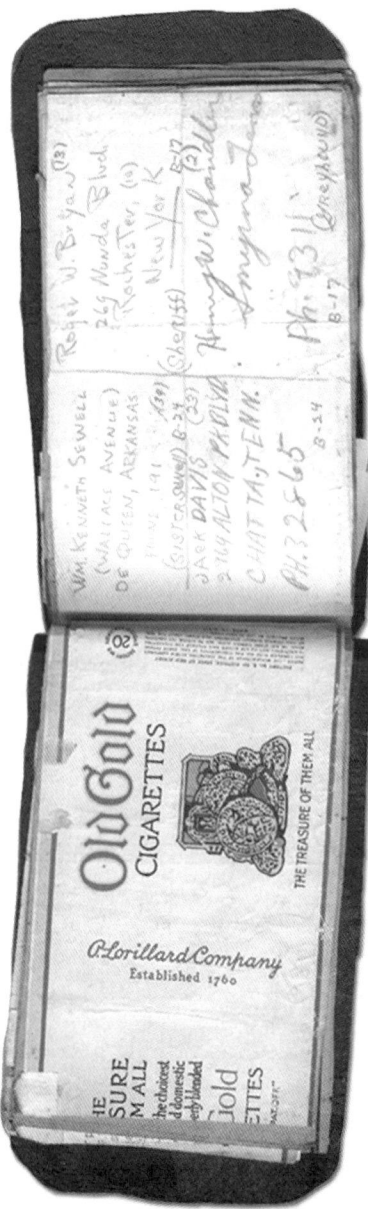

The "cigarette diaries" I kept hidden in my mattress

statement he makes scrutinized by the Germans. I did hear words spoken that lifted my spirits and gave me hope for the future. Who knows, maybe some of the German guards liked the words spoken this morning, too. Surely some of them must have faith and belief in our God, even though it does not show at this place at this time.

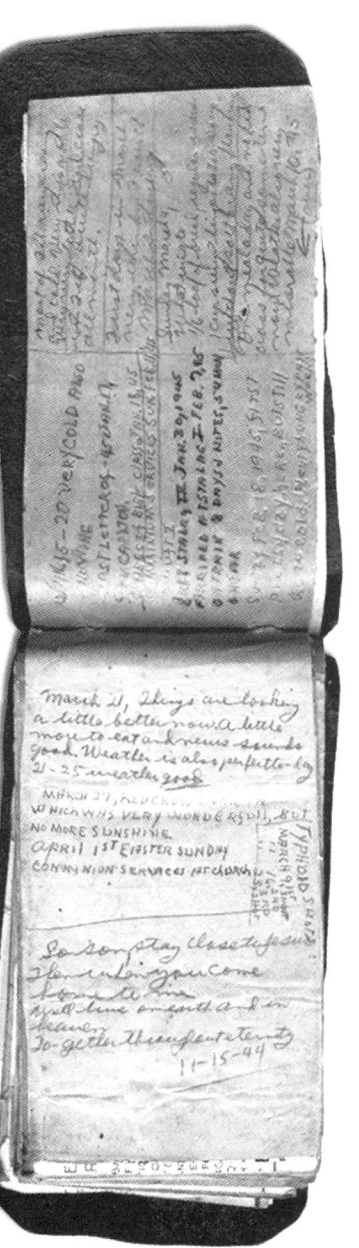

March 9, 1945

Today two British doctors have come to our camp to give all of us typhoid shots. I have just received my shot that was given between the bones in the soft part of the shoulder. I have never had a shot in the shoulder, but maybe this is the way they give shots in England. I understand that we will get a series of three shots so we will be seeing the British doctors again. I know one thing—many have very sore shoulders including me. It doesn't feel good and my shoulder is somewhat stiff. We are all wondering why we are getting the shots at this late date, but if it prevents typhoid, well and good. I am a little surprised the Germans are permitting this to take place. Maybe they are getting a little soft.

Good News

We continue to receive news bulletins that are read quietly in each room in the evenings after we are locked in our barracks for the night. The news is beginning to sound much better each time we hear something. The American and Russian armies are making headway on each front, and the German Air Force has been reported to be weakening very fast. The heavy bombing of the factories and airfields, plus their losses in air battles, is taking its toll. We do not shout for joy or overreact at this point, but when I hear news of this kind my heart starts pumping just a little faster. My outlook on life is starting to be much better. We are all hoping that the good news is true. We do not know the source of our news reports, but we do know that the Germans would be unhappy if they knew we were receiving news from the outside. The person responsible would be in real danger and I would not want to be in that person's shoes if the Germans discovered his source of information.

We have found out that there is a flak school about five miles from here and that makes it close to Barth, Germany. This operation evidently is not important enough to be a target for bombing. If it were a target it would be too close for comfort for all of us in this POW camp. There is also a small airfield nearby. This is information going around, but it is probably true.

As I am thinking about places, I wonder if our side, in this war, knows where the prison camps are located. The two camps that I have known are out in the boondocks, away from large cities and military targets. There are no railroad yards in this area and the land near both of the POW camps where I have been interned is in the agricultural part of Germany.

March 12, 1945

I have made a list of the things that I want to eat when I get home.

Solid foods

Biscuits, cornbread, corn pudding, cream of wheat pudding, sweet potato pudding, meat loaf, meat balls, salmon patties, chicken fried steak, pork chops, creamed peas and carrots (mixed), french fried potatoes, roast beef, fruit salad, fried mackerel, fried eggs, waffles, pancakes, french toast, waffles, white gravy, milk toast, boiled eggs, ham, pork and beans on toast with bacon.

Desserts

Butterscotch pie, chocolate pie, lemon pie, plum pudding, chocolate pudding, vanilla pudding, butterscotch pudding with whipped cream, tapioca pudding, banana pudding, Jello with bananas and whipped cream, apple dumplings or pudding, bread pudding with vanilla sauce, and many other things that I can't think of just now.

We still have only one meal a day consisting of thin soup made with dried vegetables and potatoes. Now I am listing more goodies that I want when I get home.

Goodies

Banana cake, butterscotch cake, plain white cake with chocolate icing, angelfood cake, chocolate cake, icebox cookies, tollhouse cookies with semi-sweets, ginger cookies, spritz cookies, oatmeal cookies, rolled oatmeal cookies, and peanut butter cookies.

Dinners

1. Fried chicken, potatoes, gravy, corn, creamed carrots and peas, milk bread with butter, and chocolate pie or pudding. I want cake with the pudding.

2. Steak, potatoes, gravy, pork and beans, creamed peas, milk bread and butter, butterscotch pie or cake and pudding.

3. Pork chops, potatoes, gravy, peas, corn, milk bread with butter, plum pudding with vanilla cream.

Man, am I hungry!

Crop Planting Time in Texas

It is almost springtime, but you would never know that here in Germany, especially if you are from Texas. It is still cold and at times it is colder than the coldest winter in Texas. It is hard to realize that back home it is planting time on the farm. The first thing the farmers in our area plant is corn and the earlier we plant the better. We are always concerned about a late frost. Frost is a quick killer of corn and if it comes late it kills the corn and we have to go through the planting procedure again. Corn has a very shallow root system and for that reason it must be planted early in the season in order to mature before the summer heat arrives. Corn needs rain at certain stages in order to produce and if we do not get enough rain at the right time we have another problem.

We plant other feed crops like maize and cane for the cattle. These seeds are planted shortly after we plant corn. After the feed crops comes our major producer, which is cotton. Cotton is usually planted from late March to early May. It is a very unpredictable crop as some years it is better to plant early and then other years it is better to plant late. This becomes a guessing game and a gamble. Dad usually plants his cotton the first two weeks in April and hopes for the best.

Farming is not easy as there are so many things that can ruin your entire crop. You can have rain at the wrong time, not enough rain, hail, severe storms, insects, and root rot. You cannot predict your cotton yield until it is almost matured. This is a hard way to make a living, but there is nothing better than fresh country air and life on a farm. That makes up for the hard times.

Farming has become much easier as far as cultivating the land is concerned since we have tractors taking the place of mules. This change was quite an adjustment for farmers who had used only mules all of their farming days. It took my dad time to adjust to driving a tractor and not telling it to "giddup" when he wanted to start plowing. On several occasions he would tell the tractor to "whoa" at the end of a row when it was time to stop and turn around. When he received no response he realized he was driving a tractor, not a mule. When we got our first tractor I was still a teenager so it was not difficult for me to adjust to the new great implement called a tractor.

A Shot and a Parcel

March 16, 1945

Today we have received our second typhoid shot. It must be important that these shots be given exactly one week apart. This means I will have a stiff shoulder again, and it seems to affect everyone in the same way. It is possible that as the weather gets warmer the mosquitoes might be bad here because it is wet most of the time. We are also close to the Baltic Sea so this may be the reason for the typhoid shots. One thing we don't need around here is typhoid fever. I have not heard of any problems here in camp, but I don't hear everything.

I have just been told some good news and I hope it is true. We will be getting Red Cross parcels in a few days. This is welcome news as our menus continue to be very, very skimpy. Food is on our minds all of the time. I am so very hungry.

March 21, 1945

For the past few days our food allowance has been a little

better. The weather is beautiful and I hope it will last for a while as the good weather makes me feel better, both physically and mentally.

March 23, 1945

A couple of days have slipped by and the doctors have been by for the third typhoid shot. Needless to say I am very glad that this is over. The only good thing about getting the shots is that it is different and it gives us something else to talk about.

We have had four beautiful days, but the weather is changing. It changes very fast here and I suppose that is because of the location near the Baltic Sea. I sometimes wonder if it will ever get warm and comfortable in this POW camp.

March 27, 1945

Today we received a full Red Cross parcel for each person. It is like a gift from heaven and the day has been saved. We really needed this food.

Easter Sunday in a POW Camp

April 1, 1945

Today is Easter Sunday. We are very blessed and grateful because we have received the Red Cross parcels and we have some food. We have had a special church service. A chaplain gave the sermon and I think he is a POW, but I am not sure. The Germans are now letting us worship in the building that we call our church. The guards are ever-present, but we can tolerate their presence as long as we are not bothered.

Three of my friends got together with me to pool some of the contents in our Red Cross parcels and we made what we called an "Easter Kriegie Cake." Here is a list of the ingredients we used in our cake:

1/2 pound prunes
6 k-2 crackers (3 1/2 oz)
1 chocolate bar (3 oz)
4 tablespoons sugar
2 tablespoons margarine
1/6 of a loaf of "jerry" bread (German)
1 spoon of peanut butter
1/4 pound powdered milk

We mixed the above ingredients together and baked it on top of the barracks stove, using a pan made from Red Cross tin cans, until it looked like it was done. The size of the cake is approximately 8 x 8 inches.

We did not receive food today from what we call the mess hall, so the Red Cross food really saved the day. The Kriegie Cake was very good, and it did get done—somewhat.

I have to be careful and not eat too much of the rich mixture in our special cake as I know that my stomach will not tolerate an abundance of rich food. I really don't know who gets credit for our famous cake recipe, but I will take it home with me. At home I doubt that anyone would like our cake unless they were in the same predicament that we are.

My prayer is that I will have something much better to eat next Easter. One Easter here is enough.

It is thinking time again and my thoughts are in Texas. April is a nice month with springtime in full bloom, and the temperature is perfect. The new crops on the farm lands are peeking above the ground and flowers are everywhere. I can almost imagine that I smell that beautiful spring perfume. Springtime is so special.

The farmers hope and pray for a good crop as there are so many things that can go wrong in the farming business.

Considering everything, farming is a big gamble. The lack of rain is the biggest problem and then there is the possibility of bad spring storms that can damage crops and property.

Now back to this place. Athletic equipment has arrived, as we had in the old camp, so now we have baseballs, bats, volleyballs, and boxing gloves. Boxing gloves we don't need as this takes extra strength which we do not have. I have been throwing some balls and catching a few also, but the spirit is really not there.

It is now mid-April and the news we hear is on the positive side. The Russians are beginning to move in this direction. Maybe the Russians will get to our camp before the Americans. We don't know at this point, but who cares as long as someone comes to free us. I can't believe the Germans will move us again as I don't think they have another place large enough, and equipped, to take care of the POWs from this huge camp.

There is an uplifting feeling in the air that freedom may not be too far away. The news is that it will be just a matter of time before we are all liberated. We are trying not to be overly optimistic, but there is a touch of inner excitement that is a little hard to explain. It has been so long and the thought of being freed has been a daily dream.

If good news continues, I know the excitement will blossom and our morale will turn around very fast. In the meantime, I keep wishing that there was something that I could do to help bring this war to an end. I feel so helpless because I can't do my share to help win the war.

April 24, 1945

It was ten months ago today that we were shot down. I have to keep reminding myself that I am lucky to be alive, but I am very concerned about the rest of our crew.

Camp History

I have found out some interesting history about this POW camp. I imagine this information has been passed down from people who have secured the news in various ways. This camp opened in October of 1942 as a British POW camp. In February 1943, the Red Cross representatives found a few American POWs here along with the British. By January of 1944, over 500 of our American Air Force officers were detained in this camp. After January many more POWs were sent here. In April 1944, there were over 3,400, new compounds were being built, and they were filled quickly. In September of that year the count was up to 6,000. I feel sure that since we arrived from Stalag Luft IV, the numbers have increased drastically.

The top-ranking officer in our camp is the one the Germans negotiate with when there are problems to be worked out between the two sides. This officer also relays information that needs to be passed on to all of the POWs. Our officer gives us orders as to how to behave so we will not have a problem with the Germans. This is a gate of communication between the German officers and ours. Many problems are discussed such as poor conditions in the camp, food, laundry problems, clothing, shortage of ventilation in the rooms at night, not distributing the Red Cross parcels, and many more.

I have been told that the Germans are reluctant to give in on most of the requests, but at least we have a small door that can be opened. In January of 1944, our camp officer, Col. Hatcher, protested so strongly about the poor conditions in this camp that the Germans suddenly transferred him to Stalag Luft III.

We have had many different American officers in charge as new POWs come in with higher ranks, and the higher ranking officer gets the job. The German officers in charge are actually

Nazis and that is quite frightening because they don't have much sympathy for anyone at this camp. I am surprised that any bargaining at all can be done with the Nazis.

In September 1944, a new barracks was added that accommodates about thirty beds for medical patients. They also have two rooms used for daily sick calls and I am told that this is adequate for our camp. I have not used the hospital facilities and for that I am thankful. The hospital must be in another compound as I have not seen anything that looks like a hospital.

With this many POWs there are always inmates who become ill and need medical attention and we receive new prisoners who have injuries and need care.

Clothing is a problem, but the Red Cross has provided most of the clothes we are wearing. They have also provided much-needed blankets for our beds. At one time the Germans confiscated some of our clothing because they said that our American uniforms resembled civilian clothing and that violated the security regulations of the camp. There are many, many unusual problems that come up all of the time.

The Red Cross representatives are permitted to enter and inspect our camp every four months. This was also true at Stalag Luft IV. Their first concern is to see that the Red Cross food parcels are being distributed to each person in camp. Many times they have found out that the Germans are just storing them. I believe the Red Cross officials have more power than our officer in charge, but we do not see any quick results from either party. Possibly our conditions would be much worse if we did not have the Geneva Convention rules. Every little bit of help is an improvement.

Next to the shortage of food, my concern is health problems. I have to keep my fingers crossed hoping that I do not become ill. We have a bathhouse, but very inadequate shower heads and wash basins. There is not enough soap or warm water to keep my body clean. The drainage is very poor as it often floods to the grounds around the barracks. Drying my clothes after washing is almost impossible as the ground around the bathhouse stays wet. We usually lay our clothes on the ground to dry. All of these problems can cause one to get sick.

The disposal of garbage is also becoming a concern. There are incinerators, but they cannot handle all of the garbage. The conditions keep getting worse because of the many POWs crowded together. More and more prisoners are being packed in our camp, but the facilities stay the same. I do not know the number of POWs here, but I hope to get a total count before we are liberated.

Good News Keeps Coming

I haven't mentioned mail lately. It was March 4, 1945, when the last letter arrived. I had hoped the mail service was going to be much better after the March letter found me. This makes me wonder if the few pieces of mail that we are permitted to send are being delivered. There must be stacks of mail somewhere that are supposed to be going both ways. I feel sure that the Germans have bigger problems to cope with than delivering our mail. It seems so long to wait for mail from home.

The war seems to be squeezing in on the Germans from the west and the east. Because of all the good news we are getting each day, no one seems to be able to concentrate on games such as bridge or other card games. There is a feeling of excitement everywhere and it is hard to control these feelings. We all want to believe the end of the war is near, but we cannot be sure that the news reports are really true. No one wants that "let down" feeling of disappointment, so we try to hold back and not show our excitement; therefore it is difficult to concentrate on card games. So I am not playing bridge and many others have ceased playing the different card games. We are just waiting to hear more good news.

The German guards are their usual unpleasant selves, closely observing us at all times. It is impossible to tell how the war is going by their actions. I feel sure the guards are being told that they are winning the war. They are still as alert as they have always been, so we are conducting ourselves in the usual way and not showing any signs that would let them know that we are receiving news about how the war is progressing.

The usual daily head count continues each morning and they are as slow as always, making us stand outside a long time while they count and then count again and again. They are not counting any better than they did the first day we arrived at camp. Oh well, this is something different for all of us to do to kill time.

April 30, 1945

Today is like all of the other days except we are all hoping and praying that this ordeal will come to an end soon. Our S.A.O. (Senior American Officer), I feel sure, knows more about what is happening at the front lines than anyone else in camp. The information that we are getting through the grapevine is probably coming from him.

When we are liberated, our S.A.O. will be in charge of the welfare and safety of all of the POWs in our camp. I imagine that he has the plans ready to implement when the big day arrives. The news is very good and we all think that the end of the war is near.

I now have the feeling that the German guards and officers are uncertain about the war. Their wish is, of course, the opposite from our wish. It must be difficult for the Germans to finally realize that they are losing the war. I am afraid to even think about what would happen to all of us if the Germans won. Losing the war has never been one of my beliefs. I just know that we will win.

One freedom that we all have that cannot be controlled by anyone else is the freedom to think. I have done a lot of thinking for the past ten months and it is amazing how much better you feel when you think positive thoughts. When we receive good news in a place like this it is very good medicine, and nothing can take the place of good news and positive information. I will, on this 30th day of April, 1945, go to sleep with these good thoughts on my mind.

Part Four
Liberation

The Goons Are Gone

May 1, 1945

I woke up very early this morning hearing a lot of unusual commotion in the barracks. The word is spreading fast that the goons are gone. The German guards have vacated our camp, the guard towers are empty, and all of the outside lights have been turned off. The day we have all been waiting for has at long last arrived. All of a sudden everyone is full of energy and extremely happy. I really can't believe what I am seeing and hearing. Is this a dream?

Now each compound is being assembled and we are given instructions and information by our S.A.O. The most important thing to do is to stay in camp and not try to leave on our own. A group has been formed to serve as military police to help keep things in order. We have been asked to follow all instructions that will be given by the S.A.O. These orders seem soft compared to the way the Germans had us walking the line. In addition to the military police inside of our camp, we will have police outside to make sure the German civilians do not come into the camp. They may not be too friendly, especially if they realize that they are losing the war. We do not want any of the POWs injured.

I believe it will be difficult to keep us inside the barbwire for very long, orders or no orders. We have received word that the Russians are closer than the Americans, so they will probably get to our camp first. Contact parties went out today to try to reach the advancing Russian troops. They need to know that this is an American and British POW camp and not a German army camp. I am glad that we are located off of the main roads as there is less local traffic.

I am still in shock and can't believe that this happy day has finally arrived. We have now learned that the German guards left their posts about 11:30 last night. They left without locking the gates and that was good since we do not have to break the locks.

It is very hard to explain my feelings after being behind the barbwire for what seems a terribly long time. Sometimes it didn't seem that this day would ever come, but deep down in my heart I knew that we would all be free. It is taking time for all of this to soak into my mind.

We are all wondering what will happen next and how long will it take before we can leave the camp. We must realize that the war is not over and we don't know how long the German army can continue fighting.

I pray that God is with all of us and that He will protect us now and on our journey home. We are not supposed to go beyond the barbwire enclosure, so we really don't feel very free.

We have been told that the Germans had orders from their superiors to move this camp, but after several conferences with our S.A.O. they agreed that it would not be moved. Our S.A.O. told the Germans that we would not go unless force was used and the Germans did not want to use force. I am sure all of the POWs here are grateful for the decision made by our S.A.O.

We haven't thought too much about food today, but I am sure things will look up concerning that problem. We feel certain that many Red Cross parcels have been stored somewhere in the area and we hope to find them so we will have food to last until we are rescued.

To my surprise the camp has grown to over nine thousand troops and we will need a lot of food for our camp that is the size of a small Texas town.

No one will be eager to go to bed early on this first night of freedom. At about 10:00 o'clock this evening the first Russians arrived and it was a happy time for all of the Kriegies. Now we know for sure that the Germans are not coming back. We didn't feel at ease until the Russians got here and we knew the Germans were really gone.

I have never heard so much shouting and cheering. I just can't explain my feelings. Now we will be going home and this terrible period in my life has come to a close.

We have received the news that Hitler is dead and this causes more shouting. We have loudspeakers in each barracks and the British Broadcasting System is keeping us informed on the news of the world. How

Cover and page from my prison diary

Part Four: Liberation 111

marvelous to hear music and good news. I had almost forgotten how wonderful it is to hear music. I need to add that the radio was left by the Germans. At times I cannot hear the music on the radio due to the cheering and singing in the barracks. We are all so happy and the lights will stay on until midnight and we will continue to celebrate. I don't believe many in our group will sleep a wink on this joyous night. It is almost time for lights out, so this ends the first day of liberation and the happiest day in my life as a POW.

Day Two of Liberation

This is a new day and what a wonderful feeling to wake up and realize that I am free. I thought I would never go to sleep last night, but I finally did get a few winks near morning.

To my surprise, things have been rather quiet as the loud cheering and singing has turned to quiet conversations between close friends. There is a lot to talk about as you can imagine. We have gladness and joy in our hearts and our attitudes on everything have changed since we are now free. What a beautiful outlook I now have on life.

Something exciting has just happened. We have been told to tear down the barbwire fences around the camp and also to destroy the guard towers. It is hard to believe that the fences can be torn down by hand, but in a matter of a few minutes everything was destroyed. We all participated in this endeavor and found real pleasure in flattening these enclosures.

We are free to roam anywhere on this peninsula as long as we do not go beyond certain limits. We must use common sense and not stray too far as we still have orders not to leave the area. I know for sure that some of our group have already left. I do not think this is a good idea, at least not at this time, as there is still a war going on even though we cannot see or hear the fighting.

A flak school is located not very far from here, as I have mentioned before. It is about one or two miles from our camp. There is also some kind of a clothing supply depot located in the same area. Several of us walked over there today and we found it very interesting. The clothing was quickly scattered and some of our men left with an arm load of military uniforms, but I didn't care to have the items. I guess they planned to keep the clothing as a souvenir. In another area we found the POW personal records of the men in our camp and this was of great interest to me. To my amazement, in the very orderly files I found my own records. It had my picture that was taken in Frankfurt when we first were captured and there was information in German that I couldn't read. This I will surely keep and hope to take home with me along with my few personal items and this diary. The building also contained many supplies and other information. There were flak guns everywhere, inside and outside of the building. It appeared that everyone left in a hurry. Who

Part Four: Liberation 113

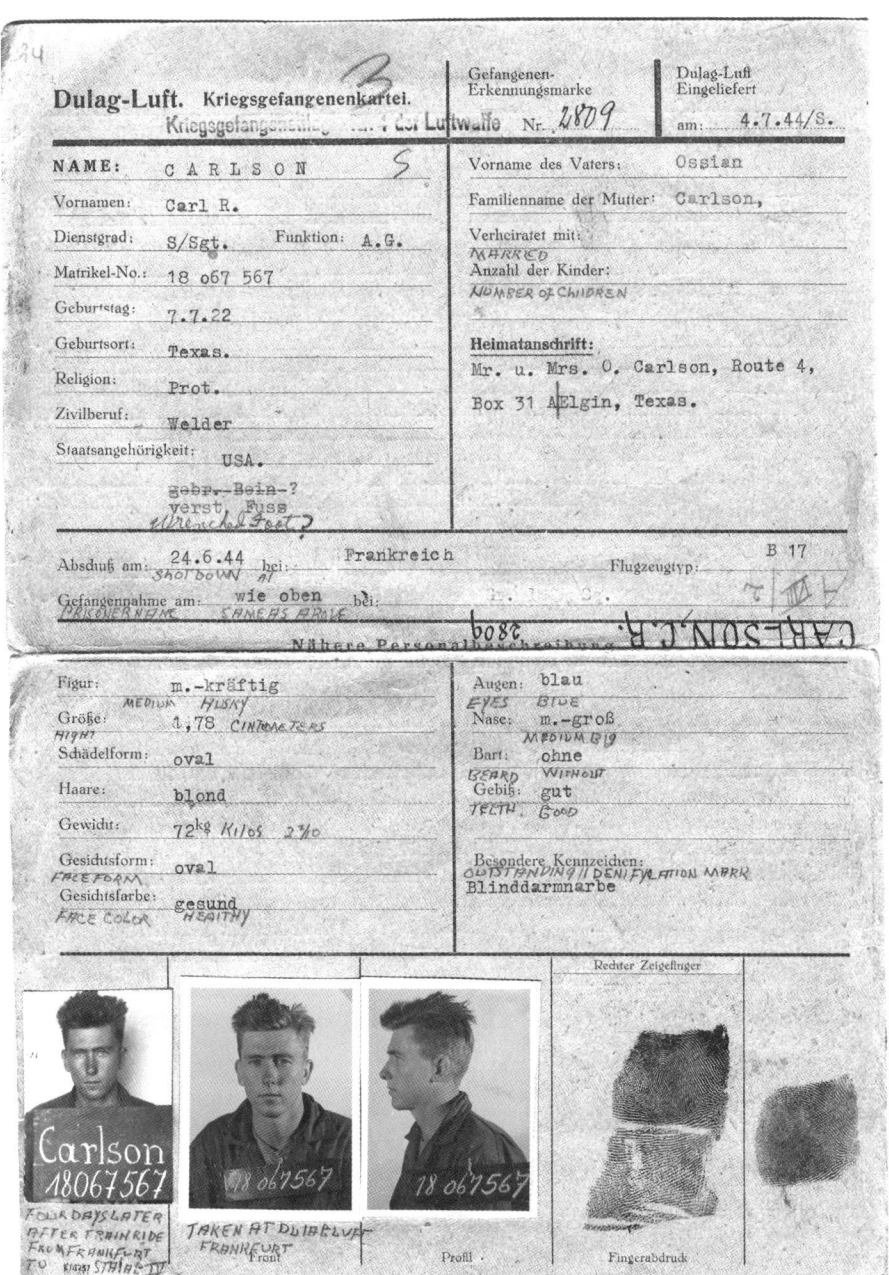

My POW record from Frankfurt which I found close to Barth

knows—maybe the German who shot us down on June 24, 1944, was trained at this location. This is just a thought that came to my mind.

We also walked through the city of Barth and found the area full of POWs roaming around everywhere. The German civilians did not bother anyone and I even got the feeling that some of them were glad to see us. We have to realize that most of the people did not have much to say about the war and we do not really know how they felt about Hitler. We saw many Russians coming through the city as this is a main road going through the center of town. The Russians were very cheerful and they seemed happy. We even did some exchanging of goods with them. I exchanged cigarettes for small articles that they were carrying. It looks like this is a Russian supply army that is being moved by large horses and wagons. They appear to be in a big hurry as the horses are always running. We did see some of the horses pulling cannons and field guns. Then came American-made trucks, jeeps, and tanks. I am sure they were on the way to the front lines which I would guess are not far away.

Most of the business places were closed and the people made themselves a little scarce. I imagine it has been very frightening for them to see the Russian Army come through their town. This may be the first time that many of the Barth townspeople realized that they were losing the war. Despite our active day no one seems to be too exhausted from walking. This has been very different from just walking in circles in camp—which is what I have been doing for months. We did stay in small groups today on our walking tour as it has been suggested that no one walk alone. I believe that most of our group followed that advice.

What an interesting day this has been.

It now appears that several hundred of our men have set out on foot in search of the American front lines. I guess they just can't stand to stay here any longer. I will follow the advice given by our S.A.O. and remain here. I feel that it will not be too long before we will all be taken out of this place in an orderly and safe fashion. As another day comes to an end, we do not know when we will be leaving the POW camp.

Day Three of Liberation

As the third day of liberation begins, the first thought that comes to my mind is whether this will be the day we leave the camp. Everyone is waiting to hear the good news. Rumors always are in the air, and the latest is that tomorrow we will begin leaving. We do not know how that will be accomplished, but we have just found out that when we do leave it will be by air. That is very good news as we are all anxious to get away as fast as possible. Going out by plane will take time because we have nearly ten thousand soldiers to be transported. I feel that our military will get us out as soon as possible. The airfield is about five miles from here, so we will probably walk to the plane unless they can secure some trucks.

A beautiful forest surrounds the camp on the north and east sides and we have noticed a narrow lane leading to the Baltic Sea which is located about a mile north. The POW camp is located on a peninsula and as I look around me today everything is so picturesque. Three of us have decided to go on what we are calling a camping trip, and we are going to start down the lane towards the Baltic Sea. We have gathered some items from the Red Cross parcels that we are receiving now. We have matches, water, coffee, sardines, Spam, and crackers.

We are now starting our adventure. As we walk down this beautiful lane my thoughts reflect on how grateful I am to go on this hike. It is so good to be free and enjoy the sights that surround this pretty area. The sky is even more beautiful here than it is at the camp. I see things in a different light out here in God's countryside.

After about a mile of walking we come to the end of this lane and there is more wooded land and then the Baltic Sea. This is the first time I have seen the Baltic Sea. The color is a deep blue and the water is very cold. We build a small campfire and heat some water in a tin can. We put the soluble coffee in the hot water, so this is the first item on our menu. We use a flat can to fry some Spam and then we open a can of sardines. We add crackers, and this is our food on our special camping trip. It is hard to realize that we are on a camping trip in Germany and only a few days ago we were prisoners of war stuck behind the terrible barbwire fence.

Our conversations cover a lot of things, but end with all three of us wondering when we will be going home. On that note we start back to the camp and the road seems somewhat longer going back, but we still enjoy every step of the way. It is not much fun going back to the same old barracks and the same old so-called beds in our same old dirty clothes. I have washed my clothes, but they are still dirty. The facilities here are almost impossible to believe as they are now worse than they were in the past, but maybe it will be only a few more days of living in this hog pen.

Day Four of Liberation

May 4, 1945

This is Friday morning, May 4, 1945, and I have decided to take a short stroll to the water just west of the camp. To my amazement the water is only about three hundred yards beyond the woods. It couldn't be seen from our camp because of the heavy foliage. I didn't realize the water was so close to us.

The day is beautiful with the wind being a little on the cool side, but I am sure that is normal for this time of the year in northern Germany. As I walk back to camp the rumors are flying that we will be moving out today. We have not seen or heard planes, but it is only around 11:00 o'clock in the morning and the day is young.

The day is slowly passing so the rumors must be incorrect and that means another day here in this awful place. I am dreaming of the day we will see hundreds of planes coming to evacuate all of us from this situation. I know the time will come, but I do hope it will be soon.

Some of the officers and enlisted men are packing their few belongings and leaving on foot. They say that they are heading for Rostock, Germany. I have no idea how far Rostock is from here and what they will do when they get there.

The report tonight is that 357 men are missing from camp and are presumed to have left on foot for destinations that are unknown. Someone must be keeping track of our numbers. This report also states that there are 28 men dead and this is very sad news. I can see how this can happen as we are all weak and in poor physical condition.

I believe without a doubt that the best thing for me to do is to stay in camp and be evacuated by air.

Even though things are bad I must remember that I am an *EX*-POW and I will be leaving this terrible place soon. As in the past, we must make the best of the situation and count our blessings. I have to stop and think how lucky I am to be free. I am trying not to get too anxious, but I just can't wait to get out of here.

The rumor now is that we will be seeing American soldiers arriving any moment. That will be a wonderful sight to see.

Day Five of Liberation

As we wake up on this Saturday morning, the news is flowing in over our loudspeaker set on the British Broadcasting station. We are hearing that all of Northwestern Germany, Denmark, and Norway have just surrendered. This is what we like to hear and we know this war will be over soon. All of us are very happy about the war news.

There is no further word as to when we will be leaving camp. It is impossible to keep from being very anxious to get out of here as we are ready for things to happen.

Something exciting has just happened. The first American jeep arrived with a sergeant, a captain, and a major waving to everyone. They are from the 9th Army. Words cannot express the happiness I felt when the jeep came driving into camp. They were quickly surrounded and the first question asked is, "When can we leave for home?" They assured us that preparations are being made to get us out, but the specific time has not been scheduled. We must keep in mind that the war is still going in other areas and tough battles are being fought. I am wondering if we will be flying to France when we leave here, as there is still fighting going on between here and France. That is all the news I have for this day.

Day Six of Liberation

Today is a special Sunday since it is the first one after liberation. I am including in my prayers the many good things that I am thankful for on this day and the days of the past week. Many of us attended church services and we heard the chaplain express gratitude for being liberated. The special service was titled "Liberation Day." He stressed that at this time we should all be patient and to remember how fortunate we are to be alive. In a few weeks most of us here today will be on our way back to our homes in America. Those thoughts alone should sustain each of us until the happy day arrives. After hearing the sermon today and all of the comforting words, I know I can tolerate the days that we remain in camp.

The Russians are now showing some old movies and I saw one this afternoon. Although they are speaking Russian it still was good to see the pictures. It seemed that everyone enjoyed the movie. At least it was a change in scenery and it was a different way to pass the time. We saw some pictures of President Roosevelt and it was quite a shock to see how old he looked and how much he had changed in a little over a year. It was a sad day for all of us when we got the news that he had died in April.

We have been treated well by the Russians and the food has been pretty good, but we still have ample Red Cross parcels to supplement our food from the Russians. We are not worried about food any longer, for we know better days are coming as far as food goes. The clothing situation and the poor hygiene facilities are of great concern to most of us at this time. I still have some lice problems and I am not the only one as many others are suffering from lice on their bodies. I suppose this will continue until we can be treated and throw away these clothes. That will be a great day and it will not come too fast for me or anyone else around here. Sometimes I wonder how we can stand to be around each other because of the way we look and the unclean odor.

Day Seven of Liberation

Today is Monday and it has been one week since the

Russians arrived and we have had only three Americans come by in a jeep. This is really turning out to be a waiting game. We keep hoping to hear that the war has ended, but so far no such news. The Russians are doing the best they can to cheer us up. Today they had a live stage show with dancing Russian girls. The music and singing were good, but I guess most anything would look good and sound good to us . . . but it helps to make the time go by. When the shows are over it is always back to the same thoughts again: When, oh when, will we be leaving this place and head for home? The answer to our question is "maybe tomorrow." Will tomorrow ever come? We want the positive rumors we hear to be true. Some of the men are patient but others are very impatient and they are leaving camp to who knows where. You are taking your life in your own hands if you leave the camp, say our officers. We are again asked to sit tight and maybe tomorrow will be the day. It is not wise to leave camp at this time and the walkers will not gain any time by leaving early.

The count report today says that at least one thousand men have left camp so far, and that includes some from my barracks. Seven out of twenty-four of my roommates have left. Some left without even saying goodbye, but my special buddies have told me goodbye when they took off. I probably will never see them again as we are all from different parts of our country.

I hope I am doing the right thing by being patient and just waiting it out here. Once things begin to happen it shouldn't take too long to get back to the States. Just leaving this place will be a dream come true.

This afternoon I started feeling ill and now I feel terribly sick. It seems others are also getting sick. We are vomiting along with diarrhea. It must have something to do with what we are eating, or maybe we are ill because we are eating more food than we are used to. I hope I will start feeling better tomorrow. Our diet is not good even though we are getting more food. I guess my digestive system is not ready for this much food or maybe it is the kind of food I have been eating. We have no fruit and no vegetables, just canned food. We have been cooking in a central location and doing the best we can with what we have to work with.

The water could be contaminated, but I am sure we will never know what the problem stems from as there are no water inspectors at this location.

Day Eight of Liberation and Still Waiting

We have just received the long-awaited good news that the war in Europe is finally over. This is another dream come true for all of us here and for the people in the free world. We are another step closer to being assured that we will be on our way home very soon. I can visualize the people all over America celebrating today. I know that my folks are elated at hearing the good news. Worrying about me while I have been a POW has probably taken a great toll on my family. Right now I feel that I am better off than my family is because they don't know if I will make it back or even if I am in good health. I hope and pray that all is well at home.

Total relief for me will be when I am on my way home. I almost forgot to add to my notes today that I am feeling much better than yesterday. With all of the extra exciting news, yesterday's illness slipped my mind.

A large group of us marched in formation over to the airfield this morning. It was a long march—I guess it is at least five miles—but we did not mind as the walk gave us something to do and something else to see. The base at the airport appears to be a repair depot. It is located a mile or two from the supply depot that I visited a few days ago. This is a very unusual situation to me, because the men working on the German planes as mechanics seem to be prisoners.

Next to the airport we saw a concentration camp and it looks like these prisoners are being used as forced laborers. They were still behind the wire fences. We all thought that we had it tough until we saw what these people looked like and saw the conditions at that camp. They were terribly crowded and most of them appeared to be starving. They were just skin and bones. It is hard to believe that any human being on this earth could treat another human in such a manner. They had no heat. I didn't find out how long they had been there or why they were prisoners, but I feel certain they are of the Jewish faith.

Needless to say, they were very glad to see us and I don't know if they had received the news about the war being over or not, but they know it now. They were filled with joy. Most of these people will need good medical attention or they will not survive. I want to add again that the conditions at that concentration camp are unbelievable. I hope the people responsible for this atrocity get their due punishment. My prayers go out to these people.

The route today took us through the city of Barth. What a difference it was today compared to my other two visits. I saw people actually smiling. They looked happy and they seemed friendly toward us. This makes me feel better as it looks like their life is getting back on track once again. I feel in my heart that the people in Barth that I have seen today are good people.

The weather is just beautiful, rather warm and the sky is clear. The five miles back to camp seemed a little longer than the five miles we marched out to the airfield this morning. Maybe it is good that our day has been long because all we have waiting for us when we get back to camp is the ugly place we have been forced to live in for the last few months.

As we arrive back at camp on this late afternoon of May 8, 1945, we have been asked not to stray far because we may be leaving at almost a moment's notice. I realize that all of us in this camp of near nine thousand men cannot leave at the same time. The departure has to be done in an orderly manner, so the question is who goes first and who will be last. We have been told that the entire evacuation operation will go very fast and that is good news. We will be trucked to the airport and then fly out in converted B-17 bombers.

This reminds me of my last flight in a B-17, but this time we will not have to worry about bullets and flak. It will seem strange to climb into a B-17 again, but I know we will be safe and I am certainly not going to refuse the chance to get out of this place. Our usual routine continues as we anxiously wait to be evacuated.

Days Nine, Ten, Eleven of Liberation

Today is Saturday, May 12. Things are the same today, just like yesterday and the day before. We have been told that we are to see the first planes arriving today to start the evacuation. We do not have a time schedule so we are spending our time waiting and watching. I don't know about the others, but my neck is pretty sore from looking up for the planes. I have been watching all morning and my eyes are turned towards the western skies, and my ears are being tuned to the sound of the B-17 engines. It will be a beautiful sight and sound when they begin arriving.

Anxiety can become very painful to the mind when it goes on for as many days as we have been waiting here. I suppose that is why so many of our men have already left camp. This waiting is very hard to take.

Someone just screamed that they see some planes coming and now I see two C-47s in the distance. It is 2:00 P.M. and everyone is shouting for joy. We see only two planes, but surely there will be more.

An hour goes by, and then we see a large formation of B-17s in the distance and we have counted 36 as they come a little closer. The shouting and screaming is really loud and I have to cover my ears. There is handshaking, hugging, jumping, and every type of expression of happiness imaginable going on at this time.

Men are already leaving by trucks that appeared suddenly. We will be going by truck to the air base and as far as I am concerned we can't get out of here too fast. The way it looks now, we will get out of here in record time.

Now we know that this will be all of the planes for today. One thousand men were evacuated in the beautiful B-17s. What a great day. These moments are the most exciting that I have experienced since being a POW. Words cannot tell the happiness that I feel on this May 12, 1945.

I am really hoping that I will be leaving tomorrow which is Sunday, and it is Mother's Day. I will have to wait and see what happens. The way I figure it, the entire operation will take three or four days.

May 13, 1945

Saturday ended a few hours ago as it is 2 A.M. on Sunday. I will try to get some sleep because today might be the big day for me. These days will be long remembered. One can remember very bad days and very good days just about the same, but the normal routine things are forgotten.

Since this is Mother's Day, wouldn't it be nice if all mothers of sons here could get the news that their sons are fine and they are on their way home. That would be a great Mother's Day present.

The Planes Are Coming

We are on standby and all of us are ready to go in a moment's notice. Packing for this trip did not take long as I have very few items. I have my letters from home, a few souvenirs, my German records, and my treasured diary. The only clothes I have are the ones that I have been wearing during the entire time of captivity, so there will be no clothes to pack.

I have just heard the good news that today is my day to leave and that includes most of my buddies in our barracks. It seems that there are not enough trucks, so we will walk in some kind of a formation to the air base. This will be a delightful walk to start on our journey home.

It appears that a certain number will be leaving every hour. We will start our walking trip at 1:00 P.M. and arrive at the base in a little less than two hours. What a beautiful sight to see all of the B-17s landing here and then leaving with loads of happy *EX*-POWS.

As we climb into the plane we notice that the guns have been stripped for this mission and there are no seats. We do not mind sitting on the floor to make room for the plane to carry thirty *EX*-POWS. What a great feeling to be an *EX*-POW.

I am having a different feeling about flying and it is hard to describe but I know why I am feeling this way. The last time I was in a B-17, we had to bail out. I really have a little fear and apprehension, but I am telling myself that the crew has been well-trained, so I must be at ease. This B-17 has seen worse times than transporting thirty *EX*-POWS. Concerns about flying should be the least of my worries, but I can't help remembering being shot down and the terrible experience that followed. I guess this is a normal feeling for someone to have after what I have been through.

On Our Way

The engines roar and before we know it we are up and away and then more shouting for joy as we leave this prison camp in Germany. I do not care to ever return to this place again. We took off around 3:00 P.M. and I don't know where we will land and I don't really care as long as we go west.

After almost three hours of flying, our flight ends and, we land at Laon Airfield in France. This place really does bring back memories because Laon was one of our targets when we were making bombing missions. Laon, of course, was under German control at that time. It was our fifth mission and the date was May 9, 1944. Just one year and four days ago we were bombing here. I remember we didn't encounter flak or fighter opposition on that mission, so it was called an easy one. We considered missions easy when the opposition presented no problems.

Our plane has five crew members and thirty happy passengers. We have landed and we are now boarding trucks to continue our journey. This is an old army field truck and we are traveling in the dark as I guess it is near midnight. As we look out of the back of the truck there is no scenery—only darkness.

May 14, 1945

We have arrived at Rheims, France, and it is 1:00 A.M. The first thing we do is to jump out of the truck and head for the mess hall for a much enjoyed hot meal. This is the first real meal I have had since I was shot down on June 24, 1944.

Now I gladly get rid of my very, very dirty clothes, "Throw them in a pile over here," we are told. "You are going to get new clean clothes." The shower served two purposes—to clean our bodies and to remove the lice. My new clothes do not fit very well, but I am certainly not going to complain. It is so good to have a full stomach and be clean and free of lice.

One thing I noticed at this clean-up stop was German POWs washing dishes and cleaning the floors. It made me feel happy to see them working.

We find out that this is a "pass through place" for eating and cleaning only. As we leave, others will come in for the same special treatment.

We have been told that we will leave in a few minutes in a C-47 for a camp near Le Havre, France. Everything is moving very fast and that is what we all had hoped would happen.

After flying for a little less than two hours, we are again loaded into trucks here at the airfield. Now we are on the way to a place called "Camp Lucky Strike."

Camp Lucky Strike

As we arrive here, I can't believe the size of this place. There are thousands of tents. It is a city of tents. I have never, in my entire life, seen so many men in one place. It appears that all of these men are Ex-POWs. We are here for processing for our trip home.

I have found out that we will be going home by ship. With this many soldiers here, I cannot even attempt to guess how long we will have to wait for our turn to go home. I think we will be here for a long time. In the meantime I can enjoy freedom that was denied for almost a whole year.

Just knowing that I am free will help keep me patient. Since we are terribly crowded here it is not really very pleasant, but much better than in a POW camp. I just wonder how they can keep track of everybody here and in what order we will be shipped out of Camp Lucky Strike.

I am not feeling well today. I have very little energy and I don't feel happy about anything. I know something must be terribly wrong, as my attitude on everything has changed. I don't care what happens to me and I am not even happy when thinking about freedom. I won't even try to get medical attention because there are thousands here that will need attention before they can get to my case. I am not bedridden.

The Waiting Game Goes On and On

Two weeks have passed and there is no word as to when we will be leaving for home. I do know that hundreds are leaving daily, so things are happening, but it just takes time to move this large number of men. The name of the game is to be patient.

There is nothing to do to keep things interesting while waiting. I am still very ill and I don't care about anything. My appetite is not good and the food is supposed to be much better than we had in POW camp. Maybe the food is the problem as I am not accustomed to rich meals. Maybe I need an adjustment period for my system to get used to the new menus.

I have found out that those leaving from our camp go to Le Havre and board a ship for the United States. It looks like

Part Four: Liberation   129

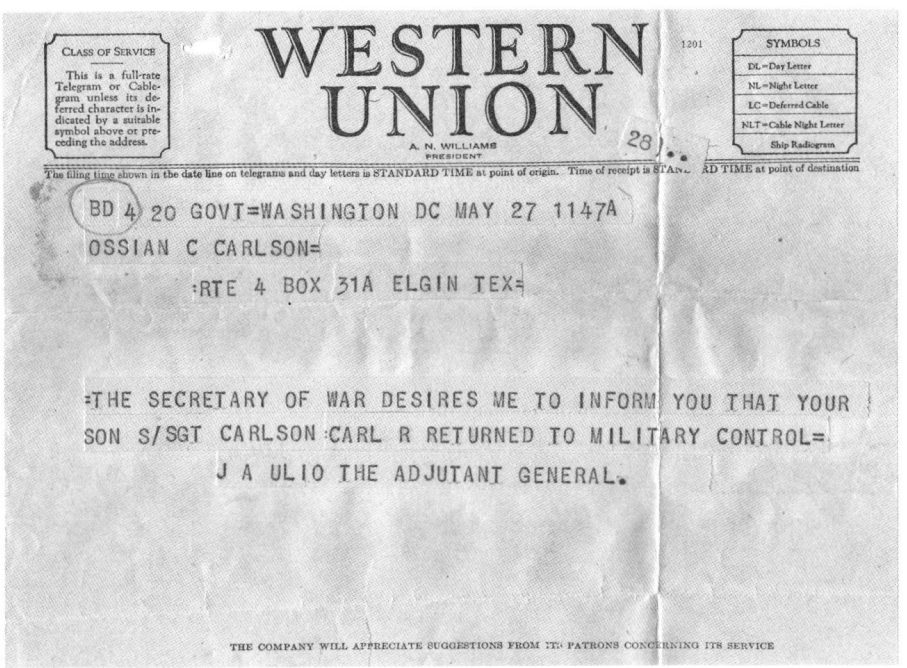

The telegram telling my parents I had been liberated

I will have at least one more truck ride before leaving France. That should be a happy ride as we will really be on the way home.

I hope to see a doctor when we get to the States as I am not feeling any better. We have just received word that we will be departing with the group that leaves on June 11, 1945, and that is ten days away.

Departure Day

June 11, 1945

The awaited day has arrived and my stay here has seemed very long. We have waited almost a month to be processed for our journey back to the U.S. I know that things would have been much better here if I had not been ill.

The truck trip to Le Havre did not take long as it was a little less than an hour on the road.

We are boarding the ship for home and we will be at sea for several days. I am being reminded of the trip coming to Europe, over a year ago, on the beautiful *Queen Elizabeth*. The *Elizabeth* had been converted to a troop ship and it was very crowded. Our ship today is much smaller, but this will be a much happier trip because we are going home to the good old U.S.A.

The war in Europe is over, and I made it through the war without being killed. I am still not well and I don't know what is wrong with me, but I hope that something can be done to make me feel better when we get to the States.

Men are still boarding and I am sure that we will not leave today. One thing that I know is that we are going to be fully loaded. Coming over on the *Queen Elizabeth* we arrived in Glasgow, Scotland, on April 6, 1944 at 9:00 P.M. and we had been at sea for seven days.

My Trip Home

June 12, 1945

The ship is slowly leaving port and it is midmorning. This will be a long trip for me since I do not feel well. I am not really excited so I know that I must be sick. I went to First-Aid today, but they have many others with medical problems that seem much worse than what I have, so I was told that I would have to wait until we reach the States and then I would be hospitalized to determine what is the problem. Each day is the same and we are very crowded and I feel bad.

June 20, 1945

Our eight-day trip has ended at Norfolk, Virginia. It is a dream come true to see the land of our country. How great it is to be in our beloved country again. When I left my homeland over a year ago my thoughts were, "Will I ever see my country again"? That question has now been answered, and we are back at home. I cannot forget the many thousands of our men who will not experience what I am feeling today and this makes me very sad.

It seems to be taking hours just to tow the ship to port and anchor at the proper dock. I know it will take more time to disembark and I am feeling terrible. During this time I have been thinking about the past and the future. My thoughts are still quite mixed, not mixed up, but just mixed. I am thinking about the time spent in the POW camp, about my illness, and what the future will bring.

The tour overseas started on March 23, 1944, at Avon Park, Florida. Our crew was organized and trained there. We went by rail to Hunter Field, Georgia, for a short stay while we were waiting for the rail connections. From that point we went by rail to Camp Kilmer at Kilmer Field, New Jersey, and this trip took twenty-five hours. We stayed there for two days, then were transported by truck to the harbor in New York City. The *Queen Elizabeth* took us to Scotland, then England, and on to Thorpe Abbotts Air Base.

June 21, 1945

My turn has arrived to be boarding the truck to take us to Norfolk and to the Camp Patrick Henry Hospital. It doesn't take the doctors long to diagnose "yellow jaundice-hepatitis." They say this is Hepatitis A caused by contaminated food or water. I will be confined to the hospital for some time and on a very strict diet. I know I will have good care. I already feel better mentally as they seem to be very concerned about my condition.

I have been informed that my family will be contacted and told that I am in the hospital and that I will be here until my condition improves and I am considered well.

Two days have passed and I am already getting calls from home. Everyone seems to be elated that I am back in the U.S., but they are concerned that I am hospitalized. I learn that I have a new brother-in-law as my older sister has married. The wedding was on May 5 of this year.

Some news is sad as many of my friends did not come back from the war. I have had good news and I have had bad news. I am very concerned about my crew members and hope to hear about them soon.

I am in a large ward so my condition is not contagious. There are many different types of problems here in my ward. It seems that the hospital was well prepared to receive the large number of soldiers as things are organized and going very well.

It has now been two weeks since my arrival in the hospital and I am beginning to feel much better, but I have not received permission to leave and go home. As anxious as I am to get home, I do not want to leave before I am completely over this illness.

Now another week has gone and this makes three weeks so far in the hospital and I am still being treated. Many who came over on the boat with me have gone home, but there are others who are still confined here like me. We are all so anxious to get home to see our families.

I continue receiving calls from my family and some friends from down in Texas and I have even received get-well cards and notes from home.

I have received the good news that I will be going home on July 21 and military arrangements have been made by rail for my trip.

As I am here in the hospital bed I am thinking about the comment that I made on New Years Eve 1944, and it was, "Will this be a year to remember or a year to forget?" I think that I can answer that question at this time. It will be a year that I will never and can never forget. This is the year that the war ended on a happy note for us who served in the European Area. Of course the war is not over for our comrades who are fighting in the Pacific Theater. The war still goes on there, with lives being lost, and there are American POWs in that part of the world who want to come home. If things keep going as they are now, I feel that the war will end soon as our forces are making tremendous headway in the Pacific Area.

I have received one of those long letters from my dad and it contained a lot of bad news. My best friend, Carl, the one I grew up with, was killed in the Battle of the Bulge in Belgium. He had been stationed at the airfield in Austin, Texas. When he heard that I was a POW he requested an overseas combat assignment. He was a paratrooper and after some months of training he was sent to Germany in late 1944. He took part in the largest paratroop landing in history that was formed to attempt to solve the stall for our ground troops in Germany. My very close friend was killed even before he hit the ground. This news has hurt me deeply and even more so since I feel he was so concerned about me that he was willing to give his life to fight so that I might be freed from the German POW camp. We had the same name, Carl Carlson. It will take a long time to get adjusted to this bad news.

Much has changed in the past eighteen months. The war is about over and all of the hard times and bad news will have to be put behind me, as life must go on. I don't know if I will hear more bad news when I get home, but time will tell.

I must stop and count my blessings because all in my family are well, and many of my friends who were involved in this war did make it back home. I pray for the safe return of the soldiers in the Pacific as they finish the job there.

I am on my way home, thanks be to God.

Epilogue

Many years later I finally found out what happened to the rest of the crew:

Pilot **George Roth** did not bail out, nor did co-pilot **Warren LeBaron**. They were both killed as the plane crashed. No one knows why they did not bail out—possibly one or both were severely injured.

Navigator **David Shoss** was taken prisoner but risked his life by jumping from the truck after being picked up by the Germans. He was fortunate to get to the French Underground and stayed with them for several months before making it back to England.

Top Turret Gunner **Burl Reynolds** was so injured that the Germans took him to a hospital in Paris, and he was there when the American Army arrived.

Joseph Schultz, Replacement Bombardier, was captured but managed to jump from the moving train. We were not able to find out what happened to him.

Willie Yates, Radio Operator Gunner, was able to evade capture.

Paul Hunter, Ball Turret Gunner, was captured.

Harry Rulong, Tail Gunner, was captured.

Glen Allen, Left Waist Gunner, was captured.

Carl R. Carlson, Right Waist Gunner, was captured.

As of this writing, four crew members remain. So ends the story of the 10-member crew.

Carl Carlson and David Shoss at the showing of the TV documentary "P.O.W. – Americans in Enemy Hands", held at USAA, San Antonio, in 1987.

Carl Carlson and Glen Allen. This was their first meeting since the end of the war. They were best friends during WWII. The picture was taken on the San Antonio River Walk in 1987.

Targets Bombed

Mission	Date	Target
#1	April 26, 1944	Brunswick, Germany
#2	April 28, 1944	Noball Cherburg, France
#3	May 1, 1944	Saarbrucken, Germany
#4	May 8, 1944	Berlin
#5	May 9, 1944	Laon Air Field, France
#6	May 11, 1944	Liege, Belgium
#7	May 12, 1944	Brux, Czechoslovakia (oil refinery)
#8	May 19, 1944	Berlin
#9	May 20, 1944	Brussels
#10	May 21, 1944	Troyles (Round House), France
#11	May 25, 1944	Brussels, Belgium
#12	May 27, 1944	Strasbourg, Germany
#13	May 28, 1944	Madgeburg, Germany
#14	May 29, 1944	Leipzig, Germany
#15	May 30, 1944	Troyles, France
#16	June 2, 1944	R.R. yards, Paris
#17	June 4, 1944	Boulogne French Coast
#18	June 5, 1944	French Coast
#19	June 6, 1944	French Coast
#20	June 7, 1944	Nantes (Bridges) France
#21	June 11, 1944	Boulogne, France
#22	June 14, 1944	Le Culot (Air Field), Belgium
#23	June 18, 1944	Brunsbuttelkoog, Germany
#24	June 20, 1944	Fallersleben, (Brunswick) Germany
#25	June 24, 1944	Rouen, France (milk run—shot down)

The Luckye Bastardes Club recognized my survival of the POW experience

OFFICE OF THE STATION CHAPLAIN S-A-1
100th Bombardment Group (H)
APO 559, New York, N. Y.

7 July 1944

Mr. Ossian Carl F. Carlson,
Rt. 4, Box 31 A,
Elgin, Texas.

Dear Mr. Carlson:

I have received the news which The War Department has transmitted to you concerning your son, S/Sgt. Carl R. Carlson, ASN 18067567, who is reported missing in action.

Pursuant to request from The Commanding General, Eighth Air Force, and in behalf of my Commanding Officer and the men of this station I wish to extend to you deepest sympathy in this period of anxiety.

Security regulations prohibit the mention of any details, however, the Adjutant General will advise you of any change in status as soon as such information can be released.

It must be difficult for you to remain faithful to your tasks and keep your spirit hopeful while you await communication from your son or information about him. But the devotion and faithfulness in his unselfish service teach us how we must live. Those qualities can be kept only as we follow his example and only as we have a strong trust in God who can be with Carl and you and me - and sustain us all. May you find comfort and help in God equal to your need.

Sincerely yours,

Glenn F. Teska
GLENN F. TESKA,
Chaplain.